At West Dean

At West Dean

The creation of an exemplary garden
Jim Buckland & Sarah Wain

Photographs by Andrea Jones

WHITE
LION
PUBLISHING

'A Husbandman is the Maister of the earth, turning sterillite and barrainenesse into fruitfulnesse and increase...'
Gervase Markham, *The English Husbandman*, 1613

Foreword

Garden historians and landscape aesthetes will enjoy this book with its outstanding photographs, but at heart this is a tale of plant cultivation. Cultivation superbly achieved through an understanding of the plant sciences. It is this that makes it possible to anticipate a plant's response to husbandry and so bring skills into play at just the right time and to the right degree. There is little more luck or chance in the story of West Dean's gardens than in the production of an aeroplane.

Garden management is a form of project management. Indeed gardening is an endless project whose living (and dying) subjects would in nature follow their own lifecycle and relate to their surrounding ecology. At various times and in various ways, skilled cultivators interfere with or replace aspects of both the plant's biology and ecology. Starting with a seedling beech *Fagus sylvatica* a cultivator may, over time, produce a parkland specimen, or a timber tree but that seedling might become part of a formal hedge or even a small bonsai. Plants are grown to deliver the gardener's intent in form and function, be they in the grounds, glass houses or kitchen garden

I have always thought of Jim Buckland and Sarah Wain as joint Head Gardeners. A partnership rare if not unique in the history of professional

gardening and possibly in the history of marriage! Professional garden manager authorship is long established from Philip Miller in the mid-eighteenth century through Charles McIntosh and Robert Thompson in the nineteenth and J.R.B. Evison in the twentieth but is less often seen today. Throughout this book the authors are shown as true cultivators, dressed, kitted out and hands on. Less photogenic lie other managerial roles undertaken by Jim and Sarah – as planner, record keeper, teacher of young entrants and public lecturer.

West Dean is a very rare survival, an nineteenth-century country house that has retained all the components of private horticulture in Britain in its heyday. A period blessed by the coming together of the wealthy's desire to own an almost self-sufficient estate and, as their libraries reveal, a deep interest in the plant kingdom. It is this lost world, a landscape developed during the influence of the arts and craft movement, that the authors have restored and nurtured. Few gardens have been successfully restored to a single period. Most, including West Dean, have happily accommodated well considered additions. If a garden is loved by its owner and well managed by its staff it will evolve. Some challenges come from the plants themselves. Time and cell division change designs without human input. On the mansion side of the ha-ha a mature monkey puzzle or redwood, once fashionable and highly prized seedlings, can now be out of scale or simply growing in the wrong place.

In the pleasure grounds overall design together with the hard landscape gives period correctness. With skill, repairs to built features can be very successful. The replacement of dozens of nineteenth-century herbaceous subjects or shrubs, now beyond their aesthetic lifespan, begs a harder question. Should period correctness stop at the genus, species or cultivar level or is all that is required to maintain the spirit of the place the continuation of overall form, habit of growth and maybe flower colour?

In the kitchen garden, Sarah's horticultural skill and Jim's fruit tree pruning and training gives visitors an insight into how flowers, fruit and vegetables were grown in the very best establishments around 1900. Visitors may assume that the plethora of plants in the walled garden area is simply a reflection on Sarah's love of plants. It is, but the bromeliads, aroids, orchids and ferns are all period correct as are the range of fruits in their many cultivars. This cornucopia was commonplace in our great country house gardens, not because owners or their cooks demanded it but to demonstrate skill, the best specimens never reached the mansion. Their destiny was the show bench to bring glory, prizes, cups, and medals.

Alongside this miscellany West Dean's collection of capsicum peppers equally follows tradition. Most gardens had a special plant group where the object was, as with all collections, completeness.

For twenty-seven years the work of Jim Buckland and Sarah Wain has given pleasure and inspiration to hundreds of thousands of admiring visitors. On behalf of all of those who have enjoyed the gardens at West Dean, I thank them both.

Peter Thoday, Senior Lecturer in Landscape Management at the University of Bath and past-President of the Institute of Horticulture was a consultant on the Lost Gardens of Heligan and Horticultural Director on the Eden Project. April 2018.

Introduction

One of the great joys of West Dean is the diversity of gardening experiences, from the intensity of the Victorian glasshouses to the sweeping wildflower meadows of St Roche's arboretum in their June floral finery.

THE AUTHORS

I am a gardener, a professional gardener, and have been for over forty years. When I go to parties and people ask what I do that is my response: 'I'm a gardener.' Not a horticulturist, a designer or a manager – although in truth I am all these things – but a craftsman gardener and proud of it. Since my first tentative seed sowings, through my varied career and hopefully into an active retirement, it is the nail-breaking, ache-inducing physical engagement with soil, plants and the environment, in all their joy and intractability, that has got me out of bed in the morning. So, despite the ambivalent response of some people to my chosen title – a combination of condescension and admiration – that remains my desired label and the subject of this book: the passion, the art and the craft of gardening.

More specifically, it is about a gardening fervour lavished on a particular place, a love affair with one garden. Unlike promiscuous designers who are masters of the short-term romance, falling passionately in love with a garden only to move rapidly on to the next when a better offer comes along, true gardeners are natural monogamists. Their passion is more of a smouldering ember than a fleeting firework, and whilst their devotion is complete it is not blind to the inevitable imperfections that are part of any beloved. We are in it for the long term, our commitment 'for better or for worse', and despite all the vagaries and disappointments that life can throw at a relationship, we will be there till the end because we are irretrievably smitten.

All of this is amply demonstrated by my particular *amour fou*, my custodianship of West Dean Gardens. However, this is not a straightforward marriage *à deux* but more of a *menage à trois*, with my Australian gardener wife, Sarah Wain, being the third partner in the affair. I first met Sarah in 1979 when she was working at the Royal Botanic Gardens, Kew and I was a student on the three-year Kew Diploma course. She had trained in horticulture in Oz and had come to the UK to expand her gardening experience, whilst I was a wildly enthusiastic horticultural student, passionate about plants, growing, dancing and drinking in about equal measure. Fortunately we shared those interests plus a lot more besides, and after having spent three years together in the horticultural pressure cooker that is the Kew Diploma we were forced to part by the expiry of Sarah's UK visa. After a few months apart, with Sarah in Melbourne and me working for a landscaper in north London, we realized that our destiny was to be grafted together, and having proposed via a reversed charges phone call (those were the days), I grabbed a one-year work visa and headed off to the Antipodes.

Within the first three months of my arrival we experienced the worst drought for a century, extensive bush fires, an unprecedented dust storm and a change of government, found jobs (not easy in a drought) and got married. The rest of our four and a half years in Melbourne were slightly less eventful but proved fruitful career-wise, with both of us gaining excellent practical and managerial experience in a variety of jobs in historic gardens and local authority parks departments. However, we eventually decided that our passion for managing large, complex historic gardens would probably be better satisfied in the UK, and anyway you can have too much sun.

We did wonder about the wisdom of returning to London in 1987 at the beginning of a recession, but after a few months together managing a large garden centre in west London, we found a position as joint head gardeners on a private estate, Lockerley Hall, on the edge of the Test Valley in rural Hampshire. Here we spent an interesting and educational three and a half years creating a new garden within the framework of a derelict Victorian landscape and learning how to work together as a professional partnership while still staying sane and married! Although we did not know it at the time, this experience was to be an excellent preparation for our eventual move to West Dean, as it presented nearly all of the issues that we would confront here but on a more modest scale. How to build a motivated and creative team and generate a shared ethos that would set the tone and standard of all our working practices? How to create an inspiring and dynamic garden that was of its time yet respected the historic framework from which it grew? How to mould a clear vision for the garden that had clarity and consistency yet was flexible enough to adapt in response to all of the changing practical and socio-economic factors that are as much part of a garden's evolution as a gardener's original light bulb moment? We worked hard in all weathers, laughed a lot, learned a lot, and in a surprisingly short space of time had the framework of a pretty impressive garden in place.

One of our original goals was to make West Dean a centre of excellence for the art and craft of gardening. An objective amply realized in the careful pruning and tying in of the pergola plantings. Rosa 'Veilchenblau'.

Unfortunately, the circumstances of our employer changed and it became clear that our future lay elsewhere.

Serendipitously we had been sent on a Landscape Summer School at West Dean College for the first week of our employment at Lockerley whilst the refurbishment of our tied accommodation was completed. As a consequence when the position of Gardens Manager for the Edward James Foundation was advertised, we knew enough of the place to make it a quarry worth pursuing. After my move to West Dean Sarah remained at Lockerley for a further three months, our only time spent working apart in over thirty years. Then, fortuitously, a position became vacant on the West Dean team, so we were once more united and with an even more appealing project on which to expend our fervour and energy. Thus, for the last twenty-seven of our thirty-five-year-old marriage we have lavished our combined care and affection on this horticultural 'cuckoo in the nest'. This book is the story of that shared passion.

It aims to describe how we and the gardens team have breathed new life into the sleeping beauty that was West Dean Gardens all those years ago and to explain the underlying principles that have guided us, the practicalities of how it was achieved, and the lessons we have learned along the way. However, despite being joined at the hip in our working

All craftspeople need appropriate infrastructure to support their activity. The current potting shed at West Dean was originally the Victorian boiler room on one of the north-facing walls of the walled garden.

lives, we thought that directly co-authoring a book might be a challenge too far. Therefore, this volume is the product of a job share, with me producing the bulk of the text and Sarah acting as technical adviser, photographic editor, muse and chief whip. The voice is mine but the experience is ours.

This book is written from a professional perspective and about a garden whose scale, complexity and resources may seem to bear little relation to the concerns or experience of the average amateur gardener. Naturally we hope that what we have to say will be of interest to our peers in the profession, but based on our experience of engaging with our visitors we are confident that much of what we discuss is equally relevant to the interested amateur who shares our infatuation with the endlessly fascinating act of making gardens.

Tree planting has been continuous since the inception of St Roche's arboretum in the 1840s. A mature stand of incense cedars in the entrance glade with a young giant redwood, planted around the millennium, in the foreground.

THE STAGE SET

All large historic gardens are the product of a combination of factors, from the physical givens of geology, topography and climate to the social and cultural variables of the rise and fall of family dynasties, the whims of capricious owners and the shifts of garden fashion. They may aspire to the permanence of works of art but are as ephemeral as a snowdrop: no sooner has each generation made its mark than the winds of time begin to erode it away. In this respect the gardens at West Dean are no different from any other with successive generations making their own contribution. Since 1603 when Philip, the eldest son of the Duke of Norfolk, built the original manor house, numerous additions, extensions and erasures have taken place in the gardens, usually coinciding with major changes to the house generated by a change in ownership or the ideas of a new age.

West Dean Gardens are not a hugely well-documented site, but plans from the later seventeenth century indicate the presence of a typical but modest Restoration garden of avenues, terraces and plats. By 1768 this formality had been swept away and replaced by a more naturalistic style influenced by the Palladian landscapes of Italy as seen by the aristocracy on their Grand Tours of Europe. In 1804 Sir James Peachey commissioned James Wyatt, the leading architect of the day, to greatly extend and remodel the house in the fashionable 'Gothick' style, which triggered a comparable remodelling and extension of the gardens. The park was laid out and the kitchen garden moved to its current site and enclosed by walls. Continuing in this expansionist spirit, in 1818 the garden was greatly extended to the west of the house in the Picturesque style with the introduction of many exotic specimen trees and shrubs and the construction of the many rustic summerhouses and bridges that continue to give this area its character today. In addition, in a bid to increase privacy, flint walls were raised to enclose the pleasure grounds and the highway rerouted to the north of the house. Both of these developments have survived and have defined the ornamental gardens to the present day. Another significant twist in the history of the gardens was the commencement of the planting of the arboretum in a dry valley to the south of the house. This was the initiative of Lady Caroline Harcourt, who inherited the estate in 1835 and who was probably inspired by her brother-in-law's development of the famous arboretum at Nuneham Courtenay in Oxfordshire.

No detailed plans exist of the gardens in the mid-nineteenth century, but a plant list of 1840 shows an extensive range of trees and shrubs newly introduced to Britain. Frederick Bower, a retired nabob who acquired the estate in 1871, continued to develop the gardens and began the long history of public access to the grounds by annually opening them to visitors. In its October 1888 issue, *The Garden* magazine described many fine specimen trees and told how 'shrubberies with pleasant walks between covered a great area and one could wander for hours finding interesting things at every turn.' In 1891 Bower sold the house and estate to the millionaire William Dodge James, an English landowner of American ancestry whose wealth derived from the American mining and timber industries.

THE PLAYERS

The Jameses were stars in the opulent firmament of the Prince of Wales and immediately set about making West Dean a suitably luxurious and fashionable residence to host the prince and his set. The house was again greatly extended and remodelled, this time by the fashionable architectural practice of Peto and George, with Harold Peto, as much gardener as architect, overseeing the many improvements to the grounds. Foremost of these were his design and construction of the 100 m/328 ft pergola which still bisects the north lawn. In addition, the rebuilding and extension of the Foster and Pearson glasshouse range in the walled garden and a considerable amount of planting and refurbishment in both grounds and arboretum (with many trees ceremonially planted by the

Successful garden management requires equal attention to both the macro and micro. The devil is in the detail and that even includes the garden bicycle and the brass bell outside the garden office!

West Dean is a Grade 2*
listed landscape whose unique
ambience is created by the built
as well as the planted. The
charming early nineteenth-
century cottage orné Lodge
and the late nineteenth-century
entrance gates are vital
components of this garden
picture.

visiting royalty of both Britain and Europe) all went to make the gardens the lush horticultural foil to the acme of architectural opulence that was Edwardian West Dean House. This glittering period of its history came to an abrupt close with Willie James's untimely death in 1912. With the house leased and a new atmosphere of austerity engendered by the rigours of war, the house – and more especially the gardens – began their inexorable slide into decline as mirrored in the fate of many other great country estates throughout the kingdom.

Edward James, Willie's son and heir, who was just five at his father's death, only came into his inheritance in 1932 and by the late 1930s was effectively an exile in California and later Mexico. Here he poured his artistic passion into the creation of a luxuriant surreal garden at Las Pazos, his subtropical rainforest retreat in the mountains seven hours north of Mexico City. Although he retained an obvious love of West Dean, his circumstances were such that he would never really live in the house again. Instead his residence on his occasional returns home became the more modest shooting lodge at Monkton House, on the northern edge of the estate, that Lutyens had built for his father in the halcyon days of the turn of the century. As a consequence West Dean House was occupied by tenants for the ensuing decades, a situation that only exacerbated the fading of the garden's splendour.

West Dean is a designed landscape and not just a garden. The continuous visual dialogue between house and landscape that is generated as the participant (owner, visitor, student or gardener) moves around the location is central to the experience of the entire site.

All gardens are products of their geology. The predominance of flint as a building material throughout the garden reflects its position on the dip slope of the South Downs where extensive flint strata are found in the underlying chalk. A detail of the nineteenth-century grain store.

THE THEATRE

With no obvious heir and living over 8,000 km/5,000 miles from West Dean for most of his time, the question of the future of West Dean House and its large estate became an increasing conundrum for Edward James. Despite his almost permanent absence the place still held a huge place in his affections, and in 1964 he resolved both its future and its function by setting up the Edward James Foundation, a charitable trust for the promotion of conservation and the creative arts and the preservation of West Dean House and estate as a living entity. This vision came to practical birth with the opening of West Dean College in 1971, when the delicate process began of modifying the house to accommodate the infrastructure of a place of learning whilst retaining the historic fabric and feel of the country house. Edward's generous and creative bequest of his entire Sussex inheritance has enabled the college to evolve, expand and adapt over the intervening decades to attain its current status as an internationally recognized centre of creative excellence connecting today's students and visitors with a rich heritage of arts, craft and creative possibility.

The gardens that frame the house are the link between the college and the broader landscape of the working estate of 2,400 hectares/6,000 acres. Historically the estate would have generated income – through rents, farming and forestry – to maintain West Dean House in its manicured setting. That tradition continues to this day but to a different end, with the estate making a vital financial contribution to the foundation's educational work whilst reflecting its ethos of excellence in the sustainable stewardship of the built and natural environment.

Inevitably the college was the main focus of the embryonic foundation's energy and resources in its early years, and though the decline in the garden's fortunes was slowed in the seventies and eighties, it was not completely halted. This process was to be completely overwhelmed by the arboreal *Götterdämmerung* that was the Great Storm of 1987 followed by its slightly less dramatic sequel in 1990. Between them these laid waste the gardens and broader landscape of the estate and forced the trustees to redirect their attention to the college's context: to catalogue what had been lost, to assess what remained and to determine the options for the future. They commissioned reports from landscape consultants Elizabeth Banks Associates, addressing all of those aforementioned issues for the principal elements of the gardens, namely the walled garden, ornamental grounds, park and St Roche's arboretum. These reports were presented to the trustees in their final form in 1989 and were designed to be the foundation on which the structure of a resurrected designed landscape would be built. However, whilst they clearly assessed the range of available options, they did not reach a final conclusion as to which should be chosen, nor lay out the route by which they might be reached.

It was our great fortune to take the helm at West Dean at exactly this point. On the ground the bulk of the storm clearance – in terms of fallen trees, uprooted root plates and levelling of disturbed areas – was complete but no development work had started. Intellectually the research and strategic analysis had been carried out and options identified. And institutionally there was an appetite for change, a commitment to a new future for the gardens and a willingness to resource all of this appropriately. We could not have had a more propitious beginning.

Foundations

THE VISION THING

The most successful gardens are the outcome of a conjunction of passion, commitment, clarity of creative vision, consulting the *genius loci*, respect for the constraints of the site – topography, geology and climate – and, perhaps most important, consistency of management. Without them considerable energy, time and resources can be expended, but the end result will never achieve that subtle sense of 'rightness' that makes it impossible to imagine a place could be any different to what it currently is. Have we achieved that condition at West Dean? On the whole I think yes, with due regard for the evanescence of that state and the tenuousness of the achievement. How we have attained that end is the narrative of this book.

No artist works in a vacuum but gardens, particularly institutional gardens, are too often subject to design by committee, resulting in the clarity of creative intent being muddied by too many conflicting inputs. We have been fortunate enough to work in a very supportive environment where the trustees and senior management of the foundation recognized our qualities of creativity and leadership from the beginning and have been bold enough to offer us a very long leash on which to exercise our ideas.

As with all traditional estates, West Dean House with its associated gardens forms the landscape focus to its surrounding 6,000 acres of farming and forestry.

Although the creative vision is primarily mine and Sarah's, as in all such extensive projects it has been nourished by inputs from many others, including colleagues within the foundation, trustees and third parties, notably Elizabeth Banks Associates and the late Tom Wright, garden consultant. The contribution of 'happy accident' has also been a significant player!

Such inspiration does not generally descend from the mountain ready formed like Moses bearing the Commandments. True insight can only be arrived at after having established a close relationship with a location based on observing its changing character through the cycle of the seasons and then reflecting on how the raw material of its make-up might best be exploited to realize its full potential. In essence this was our situation at West Dean. Our first year was spent establishing an effective team and a support infrastructure that would be the foundation of all future developments. Concurrently we were familiarizing ourselves with the aesthetics and practicalities of the site and formulating a series of reports on the various elements of the garden based on our insights and conclusions. Having been ratified by the trustees, these have been the creative lodestone for the ongoing evolution of our vision.

THE RAW MATERIAL

The garden lies some 73 m/240 feet above sea level on the broad, flat floor of the valley of the River Lavant, a typical chalk winterbourne that flows south off the south-west-facing dip slope of the South Downs. The surrounding hills are pure upper chalk, capped with a very thin, flinty soil, whilst the lower slopes and valley floor have deeper, calcareous loamy soil over flint gravel. These can be affected by ground water and may suffer severe localized flooding in wet years. The local weather system is dominated by prevailing south-westerly winds blowing up the English Channel off the Atlantic. As these cool, moisture-saturated masses of air meet the warmer landmass they are forced upwards by the South Downs, causing their rain clouds to precipitate out over the southern slopes, a phenomenon that explains our relatively high average rainfall of 104 cm/41 inches per year. Similarly, the area is generally mild, but due to the garden's altitude and position on the valley floor it can be subject to late and severe frosts. Light levels are some of the highest in the UK, a significant factor in the development of the extensive horticultural industry on the nearby Chichester plain.

The combination of these three factors provides generally favourable growing conditions but with a few qualifications. First, the alkaline soil (pH 7–7.5) limits the range of plants that can be grown. With the exception of the arboretum, it is impossible to grow acid-lovers such as rhododendrons and heathers, while even tolerant plants can suffer from lime-induced chlorosis in some areas. Second, the exceptionally free-draining soil, although a bonus in the winter, is very prone to drought and plants must be able to adapt. And third, the generally mild winters encourage early growth that is susceptible to damage by late frosts caused by the garden's location in a frost pocket.

'The most successful gardens are the outcome of a conjunction of passion, commitment, clarity of creative vision, consulting the *genius loci*, respect for the constraints of the site – topography, geology and climate – and, perhaps most important, consistency of management.'

DEFINING THE OBJECTIVES

The core concepts underlying the redevelopment were that the four components of the designed landscape at West Dean – walled garden, ornamental grounds, landscape park and St Roche's arboretum – were to be managed as a cohesive whole, thus ensuring consistency of treatment and maintenance whilst recognizing and enhancing their disparate individual character. Also, any future developments would be contained within the historic framework of the existing garden and would respect those significant historic features still extant in 1991. Any changes would seek to strengthen these features, enhance their settings and enable a high standard of presentation throughout.

The aim was to create a garden that:

~   was contemporary but respected the history of the location;
~   consulted the *genius loci* of the site;
~   highlighted the art and craft of gardening by showcasing horticultural skills through exemplary presentation;
~   would enhance and facilitate the functioning of the foundation and college and would be a valued resource for students and teaching staff;
~   would become a successful visitor attraction;
~   was sustainable both financially and environmentally.

Having established the broad brush-strokes of our canvas, the task was then to begin to develop the composition. Three important practical considerations were that we had relatively limited resources, that most work would be carried out in-house and also that we were to remain open to visitors throughout the redevelopment process and would thus need to maintain at least minimal standards of garden presentation. These factors meant that development would need to be gradual and focused on specific, limited areas at a time. A desire to create gardens overnight – whether driven by unrealistic, politically driven deadlines or by client impatience – whilst perhaps producing spectacular results for the grand opening is nearly always detrimental to long-term success. We were fortunate to be able to take a measured approach and provide sure foundations for an enduring future.

The redevelopment of the derelict walled garden and glasshouses was our priority because, in marketing terms, these were seen as our unique selling point, with their 'secret garden' mystique putting West Dean on the garden visitor map and starting to generate all-important visitor revenue. They were also the perfect location in which to show off the diverse range of gardening skills that are required to make them function efficiently and attractively. However, it was within the pressure cooker environment of these walls that we first confronted one of the underlying creative tensions characteristic of West Dean's redevelopment.

PAST, PRESENT, FUTURE?

The late Victorian walled garden was the cathedral of that cult of high-input horticulture that came to define good gardening practice for most of the twentieth century, long beyond the demise of the social and economic circumstances that had engendered and supported it. This was very much the tradition I had started my career in, but by the 1990s the zeitgeist had moved on, driven by fashion and harsh economic reality. How could we reconcile that tension between the luxury of the site's past and the realities of its much more constrained present?

Within the walls the answer is a typically British compromise: though inspired by the quality of our forebears' gardening practice, it has adapted to reflect the very different circumstances of our day. Generally we have achieved our ends by scaling down the size of operation: growing 0.2 hectares/half an acre of vegetables rather than 0.6 hectares/1½ acres; applying contemporary techniques and technologies such as the use of rotary hoes, mini tractors and trailers, biological pest and disease control and modern seed varieties; and ruthlessly culling any project that does not pay its way in terms of impact and presence.

Outside the walls that tension is still there but in a less extreme form. Here we have generally adapted our planting of the grounds and arboretum to a more contemporary style of environmentally sustainable and naturalistic planting; for example, large areas of mown grass have been converted to flower meadows. However, as in much of life, there is no one-size-fits-all solution, and the appropriate resolution is generally arrived at by an educated and sympathetic appraisal of the character of each individual area, its relation to the rest of the site and the resources available for its long-term maintenance.

THE WISDOM OF HINDSIGHT

So in the light of all that I have said thus far and with the benefit of being able to look back over the last quarter-century of trying to implement the initial plan, what are the key points that we have learnt from the experience?

~   Hasten slowly, as an old boss of mine used to say. I do not think you get to know a site until you have seen it in all weathers, lights and seasons. It follows that in a perfect world you live with your prospective garden for a minimum of twelve months before committing to any major developments. I am not particularly patient, but I insisted that we should be allowed a year in which to absorb the spirit of the landscape of West Dean before we had to produce any definitive proposals. This ensured our decisions were based on real knowledge and understanding of the site and gave our proposals a firm-footed rootedness.

~   Have a plan! Real garden making is about sustained effort and long-term commitment. The materials with which we paint our pictures are living and dynamic, and in some cases, notably trees,

Top: The visual dialogue between garden and surrounding landscape is one of the great assets of the site. A view south-east from the pergola with a range of trees planted from the eighteenth century through to the last decade.

Bottom: St Roche's arboretum was developed from the 1840s onwards. Despite the depredations of the storms of the late twentieth century it still has a fine collection of statuesque conifers including this Douglas fir.

will only achieve their full effect over decades. If you do not have a framework to guide you, your decision making will be erratic and wasteful and you will never achieve that sense of rightness that makes any garden sing.

~ Have a plan but be prepared to adapt it in the light of changed circumstances or further experience: it is a guide not a straitjacket! It needs to be firm enough to focus your efforts but flexible enough to seize any unforeseen opportunities. Gardens embody change. Trees get too big, plants die, a brilliant idea on paper proves unworkable in practice. Start with a vision but allow it to adapt and evolve as necessary. When we laid out the walled garden we designated a section of it to be a nursery area that was not going to be accessible to the public. Within twelve months we realized that this did not work on any level, and quickly converted it into a cut flower area that utilized the newly created path and bed system as laid out for the nursery and proved to be perfect for this new use. This is now one of the most attractive and photographed areas of the walled garden, a volte-face which I am quite happy to take the plaudits for!

~ Identify the *genius loci* of your site. The spirit of a place is formed of many disparate elements working together to create a cohesive whole. What is it that makes it unique? What are its strengths and weaknesses? How can you build on it to create a special place?

~ Recognize the impact of the physical constraints. Do not attempt a shade garden in a treeless site, a garden of acid, moisture-loving plants on top of a chalk down. Gardening is about cooperating with nature not bludgeoning it into submission. The gardener is a co-creator not a dictator, and when working with living materials a degree of humility is an essential attribute.

~ Be open to outside influences and do not feel the need to always be original and reinvent the wheel. A fresh pair of eyes can offer valuable insights if you are willing to listen.

~ The rewards of garden making are only earned by a degree of doggedness in the face of all that nature, economics and institutional change can throw at you. Do not be put off by setbacks; the gardener is a marathon runner rather than a sprinter and persistence wins the crown. The instant garden is a specious myth.

~ The no maintenance garden is equally fictional. Gardens can be anywhere on a spectrum from low to high input but the true gardener is *Homo faber*, someone whose relation to their craft is defined by doing. So, as the saying goes, 'Just do it.'

'A hedge keeps friendships green.'
French proverb

Framing

A view south-west across a regenerating coppice of common laurel to the clock tower of the house. The rather handsome flint and stone chimney vented the nineteenth-century heating system. Now defunct it adds an unusual vertical accent to the scene!

ROOM OUTSIDE

Before I was a professional gardener I trained as a bricklayer and worked for a small north London building company renovating late Georgian and early Victorian terraces in Islington and Barnsbury. Almost subliminally, as we removed twentieth-century partitions and the well-proportioned interior spaces of these modest but elegant terraces were revealed, I was being taught to think spatially. What had become mean and ill-balanced by subdivision suddenly blossomed into congruity through reconfiguration. I had absorbed my seminal lesson in the transforming effect of space on the human psyche. Curiously I then went on to work in exactly the same area and housing stock, but this time as a landscaper where we were engaged in trying to transform the long, narrow and resolutely rectangular gardens of these terraces, hemmed in by walls and overlooked by neighbours, into elegant, articulated and interesting areas to match those of the house interiors. Lesson number two: the layout of space is as fundamental to exteriors as it is to buildings.

Unfortunately this precept is often forgotten in relation to the garden, where people, particularly in the plant obsessed British Isles, are all too

33

often distracted by the minutiae of planting plans and colour to the detriment of structure; a bit like employing a top class interior designer to create an exquisite scheme for a Portakabin. For, however fascinating the planting, a garden's character is chiefly determined by its spaces. Just as in a building the spaces are contained by the structure of the walls, so in a garden the spaces are also created by surrounding mass, sometimes built as in a walled garden but more often green and dynamic.

Few of us have the challenge and opportunity of creating a garden from ground zero. Normally we inherit a basic framework of walls, fences, shrubs and trees. This may already be carefully designed and elegantly proportioned but more often is ad hoc, confused and dysfunctional. Rising to this architectonic challenge is the first step in creating a garden that is functionally convenient and feeds the soul. A useful key to unpick the lock can be to follow the modernist nostrum that 'form follows function' and address the utilitarian matters first. The location of functional features like clothes drying, composting, bin storage, play area, outdoor entertainment space, access to garage is one set of considerations that will feed into a design. Equally an analysis and understanding of the existing and essential character of the site, its *genius loci*, will offer strong guidelines as well. It is within these parameters that the creative manipulation of mass and volume to create satisfying and aesthetically pleasing new spaces can take place.

....

BUILDING BLOCKS

So how does all of the above relate to our experience of the redevelopment of the gardens at West Dean? My first response to the gardens was fivefold:

~ With the exception of the walled garden they were informal, relatively unstructured, and bordering on the amorphous. This was definitely not a twentieth-century garden of rooms.
~ They were extensive in themselves (36 hectares/90 acres including St Roche's arboretum) but also relied heavily on the borrowed landscape of the rolling 97 hectare/240 acre park and associated plantations that formed and enclosed the view to the south of the house.
~ Within the general air of nebulousness there were some potential nuggets of spatial clarity: the walled garden, sunken garden, pergola, terrace, house front, spring garden and wild garden. These offered a potential sequence of highlights to be linked by remaking the connecting spaces.
~ They were open to visitors and needed to be able to cater for and cope with the practical demands of being a public open space.
~ We would be embarking on a challenging and long-term project.

The practical consideration of creating an improved infrastructure to support increased numbers of garden visitors offered some of our first challenges in spatial definition. The need to separate garden visitors from college visitors meant a new garden entrance had to be created to the east

Top: It was necessary to create a new entrance to the gardens to service the considerable increase in garden visitors anticipated. The design intent was to relate this to the surrounding bucolic landscape rather than the garden, hence the use of traditional estate fencing and wildflower meadows.

Bottom: By contrast, the original house entrance was marked with a set of magnificent nineteenth-century wrought iron gates and exquisitely crafted knapped flint work gate piers.

Left top: This view of the Lodge contains so many of the elements that create the genius loci *of West Dean: naturalized bulbs, stately trees, flint-built buildings, topiary and all framed by crisply clipped hedges.*

Left bottom: The space to the east of the Visitor Centre marks the transition from the outside world to the paradisiacal space within. Effectively a garden foyer that leads you into the building foyer and thence out into the garden proper.

Right: The garden is enclosed on three sides by 2.5m-/8-foot-high flint walls with its southern boundary formed by the natural ha-ha of the River Lavant. The south-west corner of the churchyard with flint obelisk corner post.

Below: The ivy and laburnum tunnel was built and planted twenty-five years ago on the site of an earlier nineteenth-century example and adds interest and articulation to the varied spaces of the spring garden. Its base is planted with ferns, asarum, cyclamen and a broad range of bulbs.

*The 100m-/328-ft-long
Peto pergola is the framing
device par excellence. As
you traverse it your eye is
led along its length and
articulated by the regular
rhythm of its sixty-two
columns which frame a series
of landscape vignettes of the
garden and park to the south.*

of the walled garden in the area that historically had been the Home Farm that, along with the walled garden, provisioned West Dean House. This entailed clearing numerous defunct, ad hoc agricultural buildings whilst retaining the original flint-built barn and associated historic structures. Having installed the services (access roads and car parking), we were left with a blank canvas on which to impose some structure. The aim was to create an entrance experience that related to the surrounding rural landscape and only became gardenesque in the immediate vicinity of the Visitor Centre building, a kind of horticultural antechamber. To that end we decided to mainly use the native plants of the Sussex countryside.

'However fascinating the planting, a garden's character is chiefly determined by its spaces. Just as in a building the spaces are contained by the structure of the walls, so in a garden the spaces are also created by surrounding mass, sometimes built as in a walled garden but more often green and dynamic.'

BUILDING IDENTITY

As with all landscape projects the outcome was driven by a combination of practical issues, cost and aesthetic vision. For instance, after clearing the site we were left with a very large mountain of concrete rubble generated from the demolition of the old cattle yards and other farm structures. Disposing of this off-site was financially prohibitive so this debris was used to create an artificial 1.75m/5¾ft-high boundary bund to screen the area from the busy A286. This was then given a 35 cm/14 inch icing of the topsoil removed from the field through which the new entrance road curved and planted up with a mix of ash, beech and native cherry whips. As it has matured this has served to enclose the entrance meadows (sown with a wildflower mix) and has reinforced the sense of entering a distinct place by closing down views into the entrance area from the approaches.

Having passed through the embryonic bosky pinch point of the entrance, we decided to strengthen the views out across the incipient wildflower meadows to the park and to the historic buildings of the neighbouring Weald and Downland Museum, a stone's throw to the south-east, by some selective tree removal and crown lifting. Then on the approach to and within the car park area itself we used native hedges, ultimately 'laid' in the traditional fashion, which were ideal to compartmentalize the otherwise ugly and hostile tarmac parking areas and to provide a foliage corset around the private space of the Sussex barn, which was designated for teaching. In larger areas where we needed to screen, enclose or frame, we used more informal shrubberies of native shrubs overplanted with native trees.

In this area east of the flinty Sussex barn I made one of my most deliberate design decisions. I wanted to soften its considerable architectural bulk whilst creating views of the building from the entrance road and out into the broader landscape from the building itself. To achieve this we grassed the area down with a wildflower mix, defined a large circular 'glade' in its centre, and created two short *allées* coming off of it that offered views out to the broader landscape. The remainder of the area was then planted up with the same mix as the aforementioned bund. Now a quarter of a century old, these have been progressively thinned and crown lifted, and they screen and reveal exactly as envisaged.

A good example of the 'happy accident' school of design and the way that the character of a space is changed by its surfacing was the grassing down of the central overflow car parking area around which all visitor traffic circulated. This was originally supposed to be tarmacked, but budgetary constraints meant that the area was actually laid to grass over a cellular reinforcement system. This had the fortuitous effect of turning what would have otherwise been a rather harsh paved area into a semblance of a village green, a far more attractive space. It stood up well for two decades, but as visitor numbers and parking pressure grew, it became increasingly threadbare. Last winter we enclosed the circumference with another native hedge and resurfaced it with another layer of cellular reinforcing tiles dressed with pea shingle, visually and environmentally better than tarmac but more Brighton beach than Merry England greensward.

....

MANIPULATING SPACE

The transition from car park to garden is marked by passing through a gate in a low (1 m/39 inch) wall with the Visitor Centre set squarely in front of you. This outdoor foyer is enclosed on the left by another wall of the same height, which has a seating bench built into it and which is backed by another, slightly taller, native hedge; on the right it is enclosed by the old walled garden wall clothed with pear cordons. To create a little more drama and to accentuate the sense of arrival at the building entrance, we planted two apple trees on either side of the short approach path. Now mature, these have been trained so as to create a porous but enclosing foliage tunnel through which visitors pass to be presented, as they enter the building door, with a Cinemascope view out on to the park through the large bow window at the far side of the foyer.

Leaving the Visitor Centre on the garden side, you are drawn into the space by the majestic view of the park in front of you, whose impact is amplified by being framed by a copse to the south and a yew hedge to the north. The treatment of this yew hedge – which is of some age and height (10 m/33 ft) – has changed over the years. Originally it was clad to the ground and about 6 m/20 ft wide. The east side was immediately crown lifted to enable us to create the path leading to the walled garden, exposing the attractive gnarled trunks and forming a visually attractive and rhythmic feature. At that stage we retained the branches to the west to act as a screen to restrict views into the garden from the Visitor Centre, thus retaining the element of visual surprise plus the windbreak effect for the seating on the Visitor Centre patio. However, over time this crown was progressively lifted until finally it was possible to create a planted bed beneath the trees. This has proved to be a great success as a more stimulating entrance and has created a filtered view out into the garden whilst retaining a degree of wind protection. I think the lesson to be learnt from this episode is that not all design decisions are best made at the beginning of a project. As will be constantly reiterated throughout this text, a garden is a process, not an object. Continuous managed evolution is of its essence.

The trimming of all of the evergreen hedging and topiary
occupies two gardeners for two months in late winter.

Previous pages: One of my favourite topiary pieces, the river of green that cascades down the terrace steps. The winter clipping is now softened by the fresh new spring growth. Cotoneaster horizontalis *is on the wall behind.*

Left top: The circular lawn to the east of the Sussex barn. Continuous crown lifting has produced a space defined by strong verticals, the differential mowing pattern and the enclosing laid hedge.

Left bottom: A concise circle in the landscape creates a very particular effect. The circular pond in our own garden at Gardeners' Cottage has a similar resonance to the grass glade in the photo above.

DIRECTING THE EYE

Of course, by choosing to create a new visitor entrance and locate it where we did, we completely altered the entrance experience of visitors. For most of the last two centuries visitors to the private house had approached from the north off the Chichester–Midhurst road. Entered through an imposing set of wrought iron gates, the drive looped around the eastern end of the house, offering glimpses of the park to the south before finally arriving on the forecourt with its sweeping views of the closely cropped downs and stately specimen trees firmly framed by billowing forestry plantations. Today's garden visitors miss this and instead approach from what was the service entrance of the Home Farm, with their feet and eyes being led instead towards the tour de force of the Harold Peto pergola. To enhance this we have strengthened the tree and shrub planting around the college car park to the south of the path leading from the Visitor Centre to the main drive. This screens both the cars and the park and also forces the eye to the north and the inviting destination of the pergola. Here, by contrast, we opened up the view by removing an entire shrubbery and a number of trees that obscured its eastern end. We also created swathes of wildflower meadow on the historically closely mown and therefore undifferentiated space of the approach lawns. These meadows, in combination with the sight line of the mown path that bisects them, and despite only reaching 75 cm/30 inches in height, help to focus your attention on the eye-catcher of the structure and admirably demonstrate that space can be manipulated just as effectively at a subliminal level as by more visually obvious means such as hedging or shrubberies.

HEDGE FUNDS

Another area that demonstrates very clearly the 'corseting' effect of vegetation is the terrace above the west lawn. Prior to the 1987 storm it had been dominated on its northern edge by a 15m/50ft-high loose holm oak hedge and a number of large yew trees on its southern boundary. These were all destroyed by the storm, leaving the terrace like a grassy raised runway that bled out into the expansive sweep of the west lawn and cried out for redefinition. This was provided by planting a yew hedge along its southern and western end, planting a series of small-leaved limes at the base of the bank on its northern side, and creating a cascade of clipped box at its eastern end. In addition, the upper and lower banks were heavily planted with bulbs and sown with a wildflower mix that provides a strong contrast to the long alley of tightly mown grass that forms the upper terrace. All of this has matured nicely, creating a serene and intimate space enjoyed daily by our students, who descend the steps at its east end on their way from their accommodation to the college. Another demonstration of evolving design was the eventual crenellation of the top of this new yew hedge. As it matured it was pointed out to me that anyone under 175 cm/5 ft 9 inches could no longer see over the top of it, not necessarily the desired design effect. However, rather than simply lower its height by a foot, we decided to crenellate it in emulation of the

The limes and yew hedge were planted to redefine the top terrace after its destruction in the 1987 storm. Over time the trees have been progressively crown lifted to lighten the terrace space and the hedge crenellated to create rhythm and allow visitors of smaller stature to enjoy the view from the terrace to the south.

roof line of the house, thus making a link between the garden and house as well as creating a more kinetic visual experience.

In a not dissimilar vein we have developed the practice of loosely topiarizing the bulk of the evergreen shrubs that form the winter backbone of the garden into broad rolling, interlocked domes that are supposed to reflect the topography of the chalk downs that surround us. These now act as a ubiquitous unifying theme that serves to link the disparate areas of the garden into a connected whole. This subtle manipulation of vegetation as the structural building blocks of space has gone on throughout the gardens for over two decades, with the overall effect that what once looked shapeless and confusing now feels structured and purposeful whilst retaining its overall informality.

'In the middle of the journey of our life
I found myself in a dark wood
where the straight path was lost.
Dante Alighieri, *Divine Comedy*

Movement

The pear arch was added to the design of the new kitchen garden to create definition and interest, especially during the winter months, in what is otherwise a fairly level area. It is particularly magical when it is laden with golden, pendent fruit.

PATHFINDERS

Although not necessarily sharing Dante's metaphysical pilgrimage, most of us can relate to the sense of discomfort that afflicts us when we are unclear as to how to navigate the space we find ourselves in. If the last chapter was about structuring garden space to create a satisfying composition, then this one is about how we move through that composition. Just as in a skilfully painted picture the eye is drawn into and through the painting by dint of its composition, so in a garden you should be inexorably drawn through the succession of spaces in a similarly subliminal fashion. However, experience has taught me that in a generally informal garden such as West Dean – where space is not rigidly structured and highly directional – many people still find themselves in a metaphorical 'dark wood', an impasse that is only relieved by the navigational aid of a waymarker in the form of a path, which encourages them to explore.

A concrete expression of this was provided in the arboretum when we converted what had previously been a clearly delineated but rarely used mown path snaking around its northern perimeter into an all-weather, crushed Horsham stone track. This immediately became as popular as the main parkland walk, with a steady flow of visitors following it even as we laid it! This act of directional reassurance often shades into a permissive role as well. It is surprising how, in a libertarian age, the old mantra of 'please keep off the grass' still echoes in the garden visitor's unconscious, and people will hesitate to venture into some areas because they are uncertain whether access is legitimate. The wild garden, the most westerly area of the garden, was for many years a de facto no-go area for visitors for a combination of reasons, including an absence of immediately obvious interest to attract people into it, a lack of spatial and directional delineation, and confusion as to whether it actually constituted part of the garden. I vividly remember that as soon as we marked out the edges of the path with spray paint, long before construction began, people began to venture into the area; a signal had been sent, permission granted and footsteps immediately followed.

CLARITY THROUGH HIERARCHY

In the same way that our bodies have a circulatory system with a hierarchy of function and size to enable the life force to be transmitted to the body's outer reaches, so do our open spaces have a similar arrangement of drives, tracks and paths. These are graded by dimensions, construction, surface, form and layout according to their significance, aesthetic impact and practical use. Ideally they should indicate and enhance the structure of a garden, and in general the stronger and simpler the lines they follow, the better. An indecisive arrangement of paths will make an amorphous and weak garden.

Given the nature of West Dean College, a large institution operating 24/7 with a plethora of activities and service needs and all surrounded by a Grade 2* historic landscape, it is hardly surprising that there are significant tensions between those twin poles of utility and beauty. Over the years the drive that gives access from the main road to the house has increased in width to accommodate ever larger delivery vehicles and coaches, and has grown a rash of speed bumps and lighting bollards, all of which are deemed necessary and unlikely to go away. They are a given. However, two inputs have reduced their impact and improved their appearance: surfacing the tarmac with tar and chip and providing all vehicular drives with metal edging. Cosmetic but effective.

SIMPLICITY AND FUNCTIONALITY

In a new build on a green field site one has the luxury of being able to impose a design and associated circulation system in a vacuum. It has no history, no weight of received experience, and thus confers omnipotence on the designer along with a heavy responsibility to ensure that it feels as natural from day one as a long-established design. In contrast, many of the paths throughout West Dean follow historically determined routes with perhaps minor adjustments to take into consideration changed

Top: The mown path is a late addition to this lawn and only came into being after a large service trench was dug along its route. After reseeding it proved immediately popular as an unplanned route. Design by happy accident!

Bottom: There are very few straight paths outside of the walled garden. Generally they follow gentle curves that create a restful path system by which to navigate the garden.

St Roche's arboretum lies about 1.2km/¾ mile to the south of the gardens. To encourage visitors to enjoy its sylvan delights we have installed all-weather paths to ease access.

All of our paths are built in the same manner and utilize
the talents of the gardens team, aided and abetted by
appropriate machinery.

Top: The top path in the fruit garden runs parallel with the wall to the north, is visually reinforced by the box hedging, enlivened by the rhythm of the flanking trees and has a clear destination at its end. The perfect path.

Bottom: The laburnum and ivy tunnel in the spring garden beckons you to explore its length from afar and once inside its structure encloses but is transparent enough to allow views out to the surrounding space. All part of the constant conceal and reveal of stimulating spaces.

....

'Just as in a skilfully painted picture the eye is drawn into and through the painting by dint of its composition, so in a garden you should be inexorably drawn through the succession of spaces in a similarly subliminal fashion.'

circumstances. In a garden that has evolved over centuries, these tend to have a 'rightness' to their course which it would be foolish (and expensive) to tinker with. The trick has been to try and ensure that any new paths feel equally comfortable both in the landscape and to the user. Over my gardening career I have developed a series of ploys to arrive at the right alignment, proportions and surfacing of a path that hopefully will ensure its landscape 'fit':

~ If possible wait and see how people move through the site and take your lead from that. This is not the sole arbiter of a route, but it is very difficult to stop people from walking where they want to walk. It may therefore end up being a compromise between the tyranny of the 'desire line' and your design objectives. A little patience pays dividends. I can think of a couple of paths that are where they are simply because it is the way over time that people drove their tractors and trailers around the site.

~ The functionality of the path will have a big influence on its design. Is it purely a footpath or does it need to take light/heavy vehicular traffic, a grand statement or a humble byway? Such considerations will influence the proportions, scale and choice of construction and surfacing.

~ Perhaps obvious but paths do need a destination and a *raison d'être*. This might be to lead you to a particular feature or simply to connect to another route, but a path that just dribbles out into the void is deeply unsatisfactory.

~ Clarity and simplicity are vital to the success of a path. In a broad, informal sweeping landscape like West Dean straight lines generally feel alien. I can think of only two paths I have installed that are unswerving, but in both instances the dictates of the site made them the right response. Contrariwise, in the strict geometric confines of an urban back garden curves might feel equally artificial.

~ In general, the meanders of a path need to be broad, uncomplicated and generous; think of the sweeps of a set of French curves and you will not go far wrong. Excessive and unnecessary sinuosity in a path is both agitating and unnatural and should be avoided.

~ As in all artistic decisions the right outcome has much to do with your intervention being in scale and proportion with the feel and atmosphere of the area in question.

~ The gravel paths of the palace of Versailles feel like runways when lightly scattered with visitors, but are proportioned to accommodate the great crowds of the Sun King's court as it promenaded through the landscape. Conversely, one of my favourite paths is the simple double line of bricks that meanders through the grass of the orchard at Great Dixter and feels just right in that rustic and intimate space.

....

THE HOSE HAS IT

Having spent time working through all the preparatory planning listed above, I then reach for two of my trustiest gardening tools, a number of 25 m/80 ft lengths of professional Tricoflex garden hose (effectively

Left and above:
In the privacy of our private garden the paths can
afford to be narrower and more intimate but their
undulations remain unfussy.

a massive French curve) and a quantity of road marking aerosol paint cans, generally white in colour. I specify Tricoflex because that is what we use, but the important point is that it needs be of sufficient weight and to have sufficiently robust walls both not to kink and also to allow itself to be drawn out into those desirable sweeps with ease; cheap hose does not perform very well. The first length of hose is anchored at the path's 'springing point' with a large weight on it to hold it in position and then roughly laid out along the line of the proposed path edge. By grabbing the far end of the hose and flicking it sharply, you can play around with the curve of the line until it is to your satisfaction. You can keep extending the line by joining further lengths of hose and repeating the process until you have one side of the path laid out. The critical thing is to keep standing back and viewing it from all possible angles to get a true sense of how it sits in the space and in relation to its surrounds. Over the years this has become second nature to me, and using this method I can quickly arrive at an educated and confident decision. However, given that most paths once installed tend to become permanent fixtures, I would spend as long as it takes to feel right.

Another of my tricks once the hose is in position is to go away, do something else for a few hours and then revisit it with a fresh pair of eyes. Sometimes the decision remains the same; sometimes further 'flicking' is in order. Once the decision is final the path is then marked by spraying along the edge of the hose: back-breaking but very effective on grass or wet soil though a bit more problematic on dry ground. To arrive at the other edge you cut a cane to the width of the path and then mark the edge by a series of dots; I generally make them 4 m/13 ft apart. It is then easy to join these by walking along and spraying between them. Every path and drive at West Dean has been laid out by this method, which has the merit of simplicity and effectiveness.

SURFACE SIGNALS

Having got the line and proportions right, a decision has to be made as to its surface. At its simplest this would be mown grass: hugely effective when it leads the eye and legs on a pilgrimage through a gently swaying, metre-high wildflower sward; less so when it is barely distinguishable from the surrounding turf. For paths to be effective they need visual clarity, a large part of which stems from their surfacing.

When we first came to West Dean all of the paths were a mishmash of different construction methods and surfaced with varying qualities of gravel. They were weedy, constantly scouring out, a ready source of objects to ruin mower blades, shape shifting as their edges collapsed and a general maintenance nightmare. In addition, they were uncomfortable to traverse, especially for wheelchair users or those pushing prams, and became muddy with tractor traffic in wet weather. Given the volume of paths to be rebuilt, roughly 3 km/2 miles, it would have been financially prohibitive to use desirable but expensive materials such as stone or brick as a surface. Thus, given the preponderance of tarmac already associated with the building and its access, we decided to extend that usage to the rest of the grounds. Relatively cheap (especially if you lay it yourself,

'It may be stating the obvious but paths do need a destination. This might be to lead you to a particular feature or simply to connect to another route, but a path that just dribbles out into the void is deeply unsatisfactory.'

An aerial view of the walled garden looking east to Levin Down on the horizon. The area in the foreground is the cut flower garden; originally laid out as a nursery area, it was very quickly converted to its current function to which the original path layout proved ideal. Happy accident again!

at which we became reasonably adept over time), permanent, trouble free, easily repaired if necessary, pleasant to walk over, robust enough to take vehicular traffic and visually innocuous if not exciting, it ticked all the boxes and has been our go-to solution other than in exceptional circumstances. As previously mentioned, it can be softened by tar and chipping, which gives the appearance of a gravel path, but as the cost of this process is similar to the actual tarmacking and it probably needs renewing every fifteen years or so, it has not been universally applied.

SELF-SEALING GRAVELS AND 'SLEEPING POLICEMEN'

The two areas of the site where we have not used this method have been the walled garden and St Roche's arboretum. In the walled garden we chose to use Breedon gravel, a straw-coloured self-binding gravel that, if laid correctly and on no more than shallow gradients, is pretty stable. The paths in the walled garden have now been down for twenty-five years, and those on the flat have stood the test of time. However, those on any kind of slope have scoured out quite badly in places, and once that process starts it is very difficult to arrest short of relaying the whole surface. On any path it is important to provide adequate drainage and correct falls so that water is directed into the drains, but on an unsealed surface this is doubly important. To ensure that water is intercepted and does not build to damaging flow levels we always install 'sleeping policemen', a hump in the surface of the path that intercepts the flow and directs it into substantial drains at regular intervals. Nonetheless, with the increasingly extreme rainfall patterns that we now experience, we still suffer ongoing damage and may at some point have to reconsider this particular path surface's viability.

In the arboretum we have used two gravel types. Initially we chose a honey-coloured, local crushed sandstone known as Fittleworth stone. This was used on our first major track and perhaps unsurprisingly was immediately christened the Yellow Brick Road. It was very attractive but reasonably expensive, and finding supplies of it became increasingly difficult. As a consequence all further tracks have been surfaced in MOT type 2 scalpings, not quite as attractive but relatively cheap and readily available. Whatever the surface may be, it is – like most things in life – that which you cannot see that underpins the success of any path. Thus, depending on the volume and type of traffic, all of our paths have a minimum of 7.5 cm/3 inches of hardcore as a sub-base plus 5 cm/ 2 inches of scalpings on top, both heavily compacted, on to which the final surface is laid.

STOP THE SPREAD

Finally, edging – the corset that stops path middle-age spread! In general, for all drives that take large vehicular traffic plus all edges that form an interface between a mown area and a hard surface, we use our homemade

A good path draws you through the garden. Practically it needs to be fit for purpose as here in the spring garden where the path is wide enough for modest vehicular traffic, surfaced with a durable, maintenance-free tarmac and crisply metal-edged.

Left: For many years visitors only skirted this glorious meadow on its southern edge. With the recent introduction of a mown path, everyone can now experience total immersion therapy in the floral pageant that begins with snowdrops and ends in this gilded display of buttercups.

Below: In contrast to the rest of the garden, the walled garden paths are edged with either flint or brick and surfaced with Breedon gravel, a treatment that helps to reinforce the distinct character of the space.

steel edging. (For further details see the chapter on lawns, pages 173–8.) In other areas we have used either flint or brick, the basic raw materials for most vernacular construction in our area of the South Downs and therefore fitting, relatively cheap and aesthetically attractive. As most pictures need a frame, so for me a path generally feels unfinished without its embracing edge to strengthen its function as an invitation to explore as it snakes its way through the garden like a subliminal waymarker.

Structures

The scale of Peto's magnificent
pergola is revealed in this
aerial shot looking west along
its length.

ARCHITECTURAL ASSOCIATIONS

I am a complete Anglophile. Exotic destinations have their merits, but
for me there is nowhere more resonant or endlessly fascinating than my
native soil. As a consequence, most of our holidays are spent meandering
around the Shires seeking out obscure churches, good pubs, eccentric
booksellers and, inevitably, gardens. And as we pootle we always know
when we are in the domain of a demesne, because suddenly all of the
visual signifiers that create the character of a landscape have a coherence
and quality that set this place apart from its neighbours and tell you that it
has been the pride and the joy of its custodians over generations. This act
of recognition is also a response of pleasure because these are charmed
places, much of whose allure lies in the quality of the built environment.
From the grandeur of the great house itself through the utilitarian unity
of a model farm to the cosy domesticity of a row of artisans' cottages, there
is a consistency of style, character and presentation that gives the place a
distinct ambience and says, 'This is us, we are no other.' And in the same
way that combination of structure, artefact and topography goes to create
the unique gestalt of a garden.

73

All too often people's perceptions of what constitutes a garden stop at flowers and plants, which, while fundamental, are to varying degrees ephemeral and decorative. Without the visual and spatial stiffening provided by the more permanent elements of the composition – whether vegetative, utilitarian or built – the picture tends to spiral into characterless confusion that is unsatisfying in growth and non-existent in dormancy. Gertrude Jekyll in her magisterial *Garden Ornament* (1918) makes the case that the preponderance of architectural and sculptural detail in Italian Renaissance gardens was at least partially a response to the paucity of floral ornamentation available to the garden makers of the time, an argument that confirms the complementary and necessary nature of the two elements in creating a satisfying garden composition.

....

HOME FARM, VISITOR CENTRE AND HA-HA

So how does the architectural interact with the horticultural at West Dean? Well, first, it should be noted that we are positioned in an area that is particularly rich in large landed estates – including West Dean, Goodwood, Cowdray and Petworth, which are both contiguous and extensive – creating a consistently beautiful and well-managed area of diverse landscape and architecture at this western end of the South Downs. Thus, even before you reach the gardens you are unconsciously absorbing the unique atmosphere of the place as created by the characteristic flint and brick housing stock of the village, the slightly foreboding tall flint boundary walls, and the imposing and gilded wrought iron of the entrance gates. Sadly, the garden visitor no longer swings through these and down the entrance drive à la seigneur, but is instead brought to the Visitor Centre via a new garden entrance 500 m/ one-third of a mile to the east of the original entrance. Here the drive sweeps between two contemporary wildflower meadows fenced with that staple of the nineteenth-century estate scene: black painted, mild steel fencing. This is not original but was chosen as it is one of those classic estate signifiers that although humble and utilitarian immediately creates a particular atmosphere. Next you are confronted by a selection of buildings that once housed the Home Farm, including a large and impressive flint walled and slate roofed Sussex barn, a brick built dairy parlour and a charming flint built, thatch roofed and staddle stone supported octagonal grain store plus other associated buildings and housing. These have all been converted to contemporary uses without destroying their visual coherence and impact.

Having parked, the visitor is faced by another set of tall flint walls, this time those of the walled garden. Over the years of our homeland meanderings Sarah and I have developed a finely tuned set of 'walled garden antennae' that allow us to pick out the 'jizz' of such places, including walls, outbuildings and glasshouse ridge lines, an experience that always fills us with excitement and anticipation. We hope this emotion is also engendered in our visitors on their first sighting of the enclosure of West Dean's 'secret garden'.

Approaching the Visitor Centre, our guests pass through a metal

gate in a wall that is topped by a very fine and well-proportioned section of metal railings that are a remnant from the days, well over a century ago, when this area housed the hunt dog kennels. Now, in a very different set of circumstances, they assist in creating a sense of arrival and entrance, and the modern gates through which visitors pass reflect their style and proportions.

The design of the Visitor Centre provoked some interesting debates as to whether it should be an uncompromisingly contemporary building or reflect the character of the historic buildings that surround it. The chosen solution was to take elements of the local vernacular and combine them in such a way as to create something that, whilst in keeping with its environs, was sufficiently different to signal its contemporary roots. It combines the local building materials of flint, brick and clay tile with fenestration and doors that replicate the style of Wyatt's early nineteenth-century Gothick orangery and a capacious clay tile roof that, in its size and pitch, echoes the slate roof of the Sussex barn. Regardless of its architectural or practical merit, what it does extremely well is to confirm the contemporary garden's commitment to excellence in both materials, craftsmanship and presentation.

Leaving the Visitor Centre, the continuity in use of materials is immediately flagged up by the fact that the hidden stock fence at the base of the ha-ha is of the same design as the entrance meadow estate fencing – albeit original, unpainted and slightly more battered! This theme of architectural reiteration continues throughout the grounds. As you approach the entrance to the walled garden, the thatched and flint circular fruit store built into the west wall of the fruit garden immediately reminds you of the earlier octagonal grain store. This building, although practical in purpose (fruit storage), also acts as a very attractive 'full stop' to the axis of the Yellow and Blue Border. In addition, it offers an interesting interior spatial sensation – there are not that many round spaces in gardens – and for the budding singer it has a peculiarly (and surely accidental) flattering acoustic!

WALLED GARDEN, GATES AND LIVERIES

Part of the enchantment of walled gardens is that sense being in a safe space set apart from the outside world by the enclosing and protective parapets of their walls. This means that their entrances – the transition point from one dimension to another – are particularly emotionally charged. However, that charge is inherent in the function not the means: a battered old timber gate listing on its hinges can be as alluring as a finely crafted masterpiece of the blacksmith's art. We have two of the latter, probably a reflection of their historic importance as entrances through which the owners would proudly show off their immaculately run horticultural empires to envious guests. They are things of great beauty and artistry, to be admired as objects in themselves, and also have the advantage of being transparent, thus allowing a tempting glimpse of what lies beyond. However, if I am honest it is the plain and workaday timber gate that only reveals its secrets when opened that I find the more entrancing, which is fortunate as we have nine of them in the walled garden alone.

Which leads nicely into the issue of painting. All large estates have a house colour that painted surfaces across the whole estate are coated in, like a railway livery: an early form of aristocratic branding, I suppose. These may be range from the garish, as in the locally infamous Cowdray Custard Yellow that adorns all of its buildings and allows the passing traveller to map its boundaries with ease, through to our very subdued Farrow and Ball Olive, tasteful to the point of disappearance. However, the issue is less the colour chosen but rather the unifying effect of one treatment across the board, a lesson that could usefully be learned in many domestic gardens where the kaleidoscope of colours and finishes can be very unsettling.

IRONWORK, GLASSHOUSES AND HAZEL

One of the exceptions to the house colour rule is that all of the metal plant supports within the walled garden, along with the estate fencing, are painted matt black. These supports are an important feature of the space and although utilitarian in design are nevertheless attractive in their functional practicality. All new pieces that we have introduced have emulated this single-minded Bauhaus aesthetic where form follows function, and the quality of materials used in their construction ensures they are robust enough to perform their allotted task. Garden centres are awash with over-ornamented and under-specified frameworks and furniture that rapidly fall apart and leave the garden looking like a nightmare wasteland of failed consumer dreams. Keep it simple and strong!

The other exception to the monochrome paint rule is our wonderful glasshouses. These are uniformly white as any self-respecting glasshouse should be. Again this is a good example of form following function because white is the most light-reflective surface, and a glasshouse is all about the transmission of light to its inmates' leaf surfaces. They are undoubtedly the jewel in the crown of the gardens and embody all of those qualities of clarity of design, fitness for purpose, consistency of treatment and quality of construction that are central to the contribution of other garden structures.

The other plant support system that we employ extensively is the use of hazel sticks and poles. These are a sustainable, locally sourced (less than 800 m/half a mile from the walled garden) and natural resource that arguably feel so right in the garden because they are literally parochial. West Dean, like most estates in lowland England, has swathes of neglected hazel coppice scattered across its many acres. It would be wonderful if every garden owner helped to revitalize this wasted resource by buying beautiful hazel pea stickss instead of the piles of plastic tat that pass for plant supports in most sundries catalogues.

Above: The garden office, located on a less valuable north-facing wall in the garden yard, is the nerve centre of the whole garden operation.

Top right: West Dean's range of 17 Victorian glasshouses and frames is one of the most extensive still surviving in the country. Their maintenance is one of the greatest challenges facing the garden.

Below right: Manufactured and erected by Foster and Pearson of Beeston, Nottinghamshire in the 1890s, the excellence of their constituents and construction has stood the test of time. Pictured here is the monogrammed cast iron glasshouse venting gear.

Below far right: The two sunken glasshouse pits are our main production houses producing many annual crops including the chilli collection.

*We are fortunate to be able to harvest all of our staking
materials from an area of hazel coppice adjacent to the garden.
Erecting bean supports in the spring kitchen garden.*

*One of the secrets of successful staking is to erect the
hazel frameworks early in the growing season. I see them as
ephemeral sculptures and attractive in themselves until they are
rapidly subsumed by the rampant plant growth.*

This 'rustic' summerhouse dates back to the 1820s but has been extensively restored and rethatched on occasion.

'All too often our perception
of what constitutes a garden stops
at flowers and plants but without
the visual and spatial stiffening
provided by the more permanent
elements of the composition,
the picture tends to spiral into
characterless confusion.'

FLINT GOTHICK AND THATCHED RUSTIC

Nearly every garden has a house as its *raison d'être* if not its centrepiece. At West Dean it is both. It sits squarely at the centre of the garden and landscape like a great grey battleship moored in some safe rural haven, a brooding presence demanding respect if not love. The rear is utilitarian and tradesman-like and adds nothing to the garden, but the front elevation – while severe and broodingly flinty – is articulated and enlivened by turrets, towers, crenellation and fenestration and has a good relationship with the wonderful landscape of the park from whence its 'limp Gothick' can look almost jolly. The fact that it is the second largest flint-built building in the kingdom is to its credit, because this gives the house a connection to the underlying geology and surrounding landscape that it would lack if it were faced in imported stone. Also to its credit is the quality of the craftsmanship exhibited in its construction. Unusually in a flint building, the quoins are also flint and not the more usual stone or brick. To see the apotheosis of the flint knapper's art, run your eye up the razor sharp perpendicular of one of those quoins and wonder by what alchemy such an intractable material was so wonderfully sculpted.

If West Dean House is flint work on steroids, then the charming Lodge House is flint work as fantasized by the Brothers Grimm. Its roughcast flints, rustic timber joinery and improbably large thatched roof and rocket-like chimney all make it a classic example of the *cottage orné*, where gentlefolk could retreat to indulge in a more authentic and natural way of living. The philosophy may be faulty but the architectural outcome is a joy to behold, enlivening an otherwise undistinguished corner of the garden and making an interesting juxtaposition with the ostentation of the adjacent gilded wrought iron gates.

In a similar but more modest vein, the four historic and rustic summerhouses that are dotted around the grounds serve to provide shelter from the weather, a viewpoint for contemplation, and unifying architectural punctuation marks. These are in a similarly artless and naive style as the Lodge House, combining thatched roofs, gnarled timberwork and knapped flint floors embellished with the slightly macabre addition of geometric patterns made from horses' teeth. No doubt the stuff of which equine nightmares are made!

PETO'S PERGOLA

And last but most certainly not least is the impressive folly of the pergola. This was designed by Harold Peto, architect and garden designer to the great and good of late Victorian and Edwardian society and lover of all things Italianate. It is probably one of the three finest surviving period pergolas in the country. Elegant in its proportions, exquisite in its construction and discerning in its detailing, it is an exemplar of the pergola constructor's art and lacking in only one thing: a *raison d'être*. Most such structures have a destination and are connected to the rest of the garden in a meaningful way, but not so at West Dean where it sits

Each winter Anne Kelly spends six weeks giving the planting
on the pergola a thorough overhaul turning vegetative chaos into
structured harmony, a firm foundation for next year's growth.

Previous pages and left:
That process of constant
pinching, thinning and
tying in continues through
the growing season. Without
it the pergola would soon
become an impenetrable
vertical jungle. By having
two subjects on many
columns, often an earlier
flowering rose and later
flowering clematis, the season
of interest is extended.

Below: The pergola can be
read as a series of picture
frames that enclose the views
south as you move along
its length.

enigmatically astride the slope of the north lawn with no formal relation to house or view, a splendid irrelevance. Over the years we have tried to overcome this sense of being beached on some forgotten shore by strengthening the path system that connects it to the rest of the garden, anchoring it to its site by the creation of a border along its southern elevation, and rebuilding the sunken garden at its eastern end in a more formal style that connects it more intimately to its rich relation. These have helped but not completely resolved the issue, leaving the pergola as living proof that neither money, taste nor talent can always buy success.

Water

The River Lavant, a seasonal chalk winterbourne, brings the magic of moving water to the garden when it is flowing.

Water has an endless fascination for humanity, inexorably drawing us to its mercurial presence and captivating us by its protean quality. Perhaps this is hardly surprising when evolutionary scientists tell us that we are ultimately evolved from fish, when we begin our life in the nurturing waters of the amniotic sac, and when water constitutes up to 60 per cent of our body weight. This atavistic connection is given cultural expression in myriad ways, but its archetypal necessity is perhaps best expressed in the near universality of village squares or town piazzas with a central water supply. Whether simple trough, utilitarian tank or ornate fountain, these are as essential a townscape feature as that other source of sacramental sustenance, its normally near neighbour, the church or temple.

My own life reflects that unending enchantment. Whether tinkering with childhood streams, indulging a taste for 'wild' swimming or mucking about in boats, water has been central to my life, at play and at work. Not in the sense that I have carved out a niche for myself as a water garden specialist, but rather that as a professional gardener and relentless garden visitor I am constantly confronted by the myriad ways that water has featured in gardens and managed landscapes over the centuries, and these memories then become part of my subconscious image library when thinking about the manipulation of water under my stewardship.

93

From the sophisticated relationship between water, decorative architecture and complex enclosed spaces in the Moorish garden, the playfulness and sensuality of water in the Italian Renaissance garden, the dominance and ostentation of Versailles and Vaux-le-Vicomte to the faux naturalness and bucolic charm of the carefully contrived English landscape park with its sinuous line of lake and stream, water has been central to people's desire to create an idealized outdoor space.

In our more modest times the desirability of water remains ubiquitous, even if restricted to sinking an old bathtub into a back lawn. Even at this scale it can still be a reflective surface, albeit hand glass as opposed to full-length mirror, drawing down the sky and reflecting it back to itself, and thus expanding the garden beyond its terrestrial limits. And in the climate and ambience of the British Isles this reflective role has been its primary function. Not for us the ceaseless splash and movement of the fountains of the Mediterranean and Middle East. The Alhambra under the grey skies of Accrington would be wrong on so many levels, but principally because in our damp climate and soft muted light the sound of falling water and accompanying increase in humidity are the last thing we need for most of the time. No, our aquatic *genius loci* lies in the tranquillity, unity and sense of space that a placid body of water delivers. Under a harsh and constant sun this might prove lifeless and glaring, but under our ever changing skyscapes with their ceaseless pageant of clouds and subtle alterations of light quality, it becomes an animated piece of reflective theatre that brings a dynamic dimension to the garden alongside those other kinetic elements of wind, the flutter of foliage, and the play of birds and other animals.

However, having sung its praises and noted its ubiquity, I would say that in my experience the design and management of water features is one of the most difficult to get right. A good starting point is to view the landscape from the air, and the lesson to be learnt from the perspective of a buzzard is that lowland land forms and waterscapes tend to be broad, sweeping and generous in their lines and not abrupt, complicated and fussy. Nature abhors the meaningless wiggle and rejoices in the expansive arc, and our use of water should reflect this basic principle. Equally, given that water is the great leveller and will always gravitate downhill, ponds should generally be at the lowest point in relation to their surroundings. They rarely feel right halfway up a steep hillside. In the same way it is important that the water rests comfortably and naturally in its surrounding land forms, filling its repository to the brim like a classic dew-pond of the South Downs. Equally, 'the bigger the better' is another excellent guiding principle; this works both aesthetically and in relation to ease of management. Finally, remember that all ponds aspire to be dry land, and the nemesis of that much sought after reflective surface is the rapid growth of aquatic vegetation. Unmanaged, this will soon start to encroach and will eventually obscure the whole surface. As in all areas of the garden, maintenance is the key.

In the light of all the preceding text it is ironic that we garden in an area geologically hostile to the creation of water features. A distinctive characteristic of chalk downland is the almost total absence of permanent surface water due to the highly permeable nature of the underlying chalk. This acts like a gigantic sponge, sucking water from its surface and storing it deep in subterranean aquifers that only release their bounty

The flint river banks and
bridges in this area of the
spring garden date from the
1820s but were in very poor
condition by the 1990s. They
were rebuilt during the river's
dry periods by the garden
staff over a number of years.

Top and bottom: When the river
dries up it leaves a deposit of
silt on the flinted riverbed which
would very quickly obscure it if
this were not removed annually.
A rather smelly job but one
which highlights the attention
to detailed maintenance that
is required to keep a dynamic
entity such as a garden in a
relatively stable state. Once
cleaned the dry riverbed then
becomes an attractive feature
in itself.

when the water table rises sufficiently for the numerous springs in the gentle dry valley bottoms to burst. Only then do those elusive miracles of chalk hydrology appear, the ephemeral but therefore particularly alluring winterbournes. These intermittent seasonal watercourses are almost totally dependent on the recharging of the chalk aquifers by rainfall, with surface run-off playing a negligible role.

Our own River Lavant, which rises a couple of miles to the north of West Dean and discharges into the sea in Chichester Harbour, has amply demonstrated its chameleon-like character in our twenty-seven years by flooding Chichester twice, flowing all year round once, and in other years barely flowing at all. However, its normal pattern is to rise in December or January, rapidly build to a crescendo, and then run with diminishing vigour until finally drying in July or August. Once this has happened we are faced with a litany of accusatory questions along the lines of 'What have you done with the river?' – which demonstrates a touching faith in our omnipotence and a poor grasp of the hydrology of chalk streams. These questions are frequently followed by the helpful suggestion that we might like to engage in some Soviet-style mega-manipulation of the natural world, in total denial of its inherent character, and thus by some aqueous alchemy turn our seasonal winterbourne into a permanent watercourse. At this juncture we gently point out that, unless you are a totalitarian dictator, satisfying landscape outcomes are generally best achieved by working with the grain of the environment rather than against it.

Personally I love the enigma of a disappearing river and eagerly await its annual reappearance with the same sense of anticipation as the return of our swallows. We can predict the river's rise scientifically by referring back to records of the correlation between the rise of the water in our well and the flow of the river. More empirically we can simply observe the welling of the water in 'Harold's Hole', named for a long departed gardener, which is the lowest point of the riverbed within the grounds. Counter-intuitively the embryonic river slowly fills this hollow and then begins to creep steadily back upstream, becoming more vigorous as steadily more and more springs break along the river's course. Eventually they all coalesce to form a quicksilver ribbon that snakes coastward, once more enlivening the gardens and valley with its glittering presence.

Whilst the river is a natural phenomenon, it has been manipulated over time to perform a number of specific roles within the garden. At the eastern end it forms the garden's southern boundary, separating it from the landscape park beyond. This is an interface whose aim of seamless visual continuity from house to park has normally been achieved by that scenic sleight of hand of the eighteenth-century landscape movement, the ha-ha. In the past this feature was created at West Dean by having a low fence set at the base of the river's northern bank. This excluded the stock from the grounds yet was invisible when viewed from the house. Unfortunately at some point the space between bank and fence was backfilled with dredgings from the riverbed, causing the fence to slowly collapse and thereby creating a major stock control and landscape problem. To remedy this issue the fence was taken down, repaired and reinstated whilst the bank was regraded to its original configuration and reseeded, thus allowing easy maintenance with a Flymo mower whilst still concealing the offending fence. This maintained the uninterrupted view,

'Our aquatic *genius loci* lies in the tranquillity, unity and sense of space that a placid body of water delivers and which, under our ever changing skies, becomes an animated piece of reflective theatre.'

Building a new 'rustic' bridge over the short tributary
that bisects the spring garden.

gave the fence another few decades of life, and left us with a sustainable and attractive feature, a successful outcome that has driven much of the other restoration work on the riverbed and banks.

At the western end of the garden the river changes course to flow through the body of the grounds to form a linear feature from which the surrounding areas draw their character. Within the spring garden, an area originally developed in the 1810–20 period, the river course was flint lined and controlled by a series of weirs and sluices. These were crossed by a number of bridges made from flint and tufa-like Bognor Rock, a local stone quarried from the Bognor foreshore in earlier centuries. Combined with the surrounding rustic summerhouses and rockeries, they formed an ensemble in a very distinctive style christened late Regency Grotesque. Sadly the depredations of weather and flood meant that most of these features were either derelict, buried beneath a deep mantle of silt, or obscured by encroaching vegetation. Over a decade the vegetation was cleared, the watercourses excavated and all of the flint and stonework features rebuilt, a process made simpler by the river's 'now you see it, now you don't' nature.

In my view the weirs have a dual function: primarily to regulate the flow and height of the river but secondarily to create aural and visual stimulation as the water is animated and enlivened as it flows over their heavily rusticated flint slopes. They serve as a sort of nineteenth-century rustic English variation on the chadars of the Mughal gardens of Kashmir and are an excellent device to introduce sound and sparkle into any water feature anywhere. A less desirable outcome of the weirs is to cause deposition of suspended sediment in the calm stretches of water upstream of them. Unmanaged, these carefully restored riverbeds would soon disappear under another thick layer of river silt if every year we did not spend a muddy couple of days removing this ooze after the river has dried. Once completed, this simple act of maintenance transforms the riverbed into a waterless but attractive feature in itself – a little like the dry pebble riverbeds seen in classical Japanese gardens. As always, timely maintenance pays dividends.

In other stretches of the riverbed, particularly the two tributaries that were suffering from collapsing banks and heavy silting, the bed was dug out, regraded and surfaced using a relatively coarse gravel, and then the banks were redefined, regraded and stabilized with low embankments made from a local sandstone. The result has transfigured two unkempt, unattractive and unmaintainable areas into one of the most appreciated parts of the garden. It draws people to the sound of running water, the play of reflective light, and the pleasure of the new and varied associated riverside plantings. Of course, not everyone is fortunate enough to have a winterbourne running through their garden, but on a smaller scale and in a more urban setting a similar effect can be achieved with a rill or swale.

Finally, the only part of the grounds where I had ever seen water standing was at the most westerly end of the gardens, in the area known as the wild garden. This was a piece of woodland garden almost completely destroyed by the Great Storm of 1987. For a number of years it remained derelict, and the first stage in its reinstatement was to create a circulatory path system that would provide easy access. However, this in itself was not enough to draw people to this distant outpost; what was needed was a 'honeypot'. In the absence of any permanent water within the garden and

'Personally I love the enigma of a disappearing river and eagerly await its annual reappearance with the same sense of anticipation as the return of our swallows.'

The wild garden tributary, created in the 1890s
to bring the river through the west end of the garden,
was the last to be restored.

recognizing the pulling power of a pond, we decided to create a relatively large natural pool on the approximate site of the seasonal puddle that appeared after heavy winter rain. Given that this area was virtually pure gravel overlying chalk bedrock, we knew a permanent water feature would require a butyl liner. Having excavated the pond, a large kidney shape 30 m/100 ft × 15 m/50 ft and varying from 2 m/7 ft deep in its centre to 6 cm/2½ inches at its margins, we built a low breeze-block wall to support the pond edge, the liner was installed (an art in itself) and the pool filled. Despite sitting naked in an expansive surrounding of bare gravelly soil, three things were immediately evident. First, it looked just right, confirming the choice of location. Two, it was instantly covered in noisy wildfowl, the bulk of whom stayed a few days and then disappeared from whence they had come. And, three, people immediately came to sit and stare. It was a success.

The pond has been in place for well over a decade now, and the only maintenance required has been the biennial trimming back of the marginal vegetation. Remember the mantra, 'All ponds aspire to be dry land.' Without that regular haircut our lovely, vegetation framed, reflective mirror would soon be lost to sight beneath a mat of rampant aquatics. A snip in time saves nine!

> 'Land, then, is not merely soil; it is a fountain of energy
> flowing through a circuit of soil, plants and animals.'
> Aldo Leopold, ecologist

Soils

*Virtually all of our green
waste is recycled. All woody
arisings are chipped, stacked
for at least six months and
then used as a mulch.*

Even as a child and long before any nascent horticultural urges had germinated, I was always fascinated by the world of soil. Whether creeping around beneath the veil of bracken that dominated the sandy soils of the common by my grandparents' rural Essex home or digging simulated First World War dug-outs into the plasticine-like clay soils of my parents' north London garden, it always seemed to be a thing of tactility and reassuring solidity. As my engagement with it moved from play to purposeful production, in an arc from dug-outs to double digging, my childhood intuition was confirmed: the answer really did lie in the soil! Sadly, that truism belies the fact that this most miraculous of materials is one of the most misunderstood, mismanaged and undervalued of all of the support systems that sustain life on earth.

The nature and condition of your soil is one of the factors which will define the character of any garden, so it is a good idea to become familiar with its qualities and challenges as soon as possible. Prior to coming to West Dean I had principally gardened on neutral to acid clay soils, whether in smoggy London, bucolic Hampshire or sunny Melbourne. These were fertile and moisture retentive but intractable for large parts of the year: superglue in the winter, brick-like in the summer. Moving to the South Downs introduced me to a new soil type, a gravelly, alkaline loam

overlying great depths of pure, brilliant white chalk, less fertile
but astonishingly free draining and quite workable even after heavy
rain. So two soils of almost opposite qualities but united in the fact that
they were both readily improved by the addition of copious quantities
of organic matter in whatever form it was available, whether compost,
well-rotted manure or composted woodchip.

THE APPLIANCE OF SCIENCE

Now why should that be so? To answer that question I think we first
need to establish a few basic principles of soil science. Bear with
me, you will not regret it. The holy grail of soils – a deep, moisture-
retentive but free-draining loam – enjoys that status because it is
the most user-friendly soil type and in theory enables you to grow
the broadest spectrum of plants. It is also de rigueur if you want to
indulge in the horticultural one-upmanship of growing prize-winning
pumpkins or any other poor plant that can be pumped up to skin-
splitting proportions on a diet of loamy chocolate cake stuffed full of
botanical dietary supplements.

It can produce such feats of productivity because it has the perfect
structure to supply the three requirements that plants need from soil:
water, air and nutrition. Plant growth suffers when any of these are
absent or out of balance. Too much air equals drought and wilting, too
much moisture equals waterlogging and drowning, and if the nutrient
supply is unbalanced plants either starve or put on excessive, 'flabby'
growth susceptible to pest and disease attack or physical collapse.

TEXTURE

All soils are made up of two key components – mineral and organic.
In most cultivated soils the mineral content forms their framework and
exerts a major influence on their characteristics. Soil texture describes
the mineral composition and is usually defined as the relative proportions
of sand, silt and clay particles. These particles range from relatively large
in sandy soils (gritty to the touch), to tiny in clays (sticky), with silts
(often described as soapy) falling between the two.

In general, fine-textured soils such as clays, clay loam, silts and fine
sands have good water retention but poor drainage. In contrast, coarse-
textured soils like coarse sands and sandy loams are well drained but
droughty. This also has a knock-on effect on soil temperatures and
therefore plant growth, as it takes more energy to heat up wet soil than
the same volume of dry soil. Thus, in the spring, well-drained coarse
sands warm up more rapidly than other soil types. This is equally true
of those with a higher organic content due to their darker colour and
therefore greater capacity to absorb heat.

In the same vein, soils with a high clay content continue to release
nutrients as they weather and thus have good nutrient retention. In
contrast, sands have poor nutrient retention as they are mostly inert

*Top: The soil at West Dean
can vary from virtually a
gravel pit on the front lawn,
through a light, gravelly
alkaline loam of up to 0.5 m/
2 ft deep on the lower slopes
to a very thin skin of 75–150
mm/3–6 in on the upper
slopes.*

*Bottom: Underlying all of the
above are vast deposits of pure
chalk marbled with bands
of flint. This defines the
topography, hydrology and
ecology of the site. Geology is
gardening destiny!*

Given the lean and hungry nature of our soil it is virtually impossible to add too much organic matter to it. All new planting areas are normally allowed to remain fallow for at least one year and copious amounts of compost incorporated prior to planting.

and any nutrients that are present are readily leached by rapid drainage: hence their description as 'hungry soils'. This textural difference also governs the amount of effort required to cultivate different types, with the finer particled clays and silts being known as 'heavy' and the coarser particled sands as 'light', a division that anyone who has had to hand-dig heavy clay soils will verify with feeling.

STRUCTURE

A soil's texture also influences its structure and therefore its fertility, tractability and suitability for growing plants. If texture is about the size and type of soil particles, structure is about how these individual units are arranged en masse.

In order to provide a suitable root environment for plant growth, soil must be aggregated in such a way as to ensure:

~ good gaseous exchange: the intake of oxygen and expulsion of carbon dioxide – without it the plant's respiration and therefore growth is impaired;
~ optimum reserves of water;
~ a high water infiltration rate, to prevent damaging excess surface runoff;
~ good drainage: free downward movement of water;
~ an interconnected network of spaces to facilitate root exploration for moisture and nutrients.

Plant roots and soil organisms live in the pores between the solid components of a soil in the same way that we inhabit the spaces created by the walls of our houses. The critical factor in evaluating the character of a soil is the quality of these spaces. Too large, too small or too homogenous all cause problems. In an ideal garden soil the particles are aggregated in such a way as to create 'crumbs'. The interior of a soil crumb consists of many small pores that hold water against the pull of gravity whilst the bigger gaps between the crumbs allow gravitational pull to drain the pores. Thus, after being fully wetted and allowed to drain, there will be mainly water within the crumbs and mainly air between them – perfect for both plant growth and the beneficial soil flora and fauna that support it.

HUMUS AND TILTH

So, having identified a desirable soil's constitution, we can return to the original question of why the addition of organic matter to most soils has such positive benefits. Unsurprisingly, much of it relates to the aforementioned, all-important crumb structure. When fresh well-rotted compost or manure is added it physically opens up the soil, increasing aeration and drainage. Then, as it breaks down, the residue of jelly-like humus formed from its decomposition acts as a loamy superglue.

113

*The winter woodchip mulching programme in full swing. Without
consistent mulching we would be unable to maintain
our high standards of presentation.*

This assists in the aggregation of soil particles into crumbs, enabling the gardener to produce the much desired 'crumbly tilth', beloved of all vegetable growing manuals, as a seedbed. In addition, the humus also acts as a botanical pick-me-up, slowly releasing plant nutrients that would otherwise be lost through the leaching effect of moisture.

THE LIVING SOIL

A healthy soil is not just a well-structured but totally inert system. It is also a dizzyingly complex ecosystem of living organisms including fungi, bacteria and earthworms, all of which play a variety of roles in any soil's capacity to support both plant life and itself in a sustainable fashion. These include assisting in the decomposition of organic matter to release mineral nutrients and form humus, opening up the soil by their tunnelling action and fixing gaseous nitrogen to become available to plant roots. However, to function and provide these benefits they themselves need a food source, and this is principally supplied by organic matter: another reason why it is so crucial in maintaining a healthy, well-structured soil.

ORGANIC MATTER

Having established the science and desirability of organic matter as a soil additive, how does one go about ensuring a supply of the life-enhancing right stuff? The obvious division is between buying it in or producing your own, with most of us probably doing a bit of both. As a matter of principle, all gardens should aspire to being closed and self-sufficient systems emulating natural ecosystems that are sustainable over millennia if undisturbed. Realistically, for most of us this will be an aspiration rather than a reality but a worthy one nonetheless.

Over the years our practice has changed. For our first two decades we had an in-house farming operation with dairy herds and other livestock, and as a consequence had a ready supply of cheap, strawy manure supplied in bulk to our compost yard. This was generally delivered in early spring, when the cattle sheds in which the stock had overwintered were cleared and cleaned. It was then stacked in a large heap, turned occasionally and left to rot for the summer to be used over the following autumn and winter, by which time it was well rotted and like rich chocolate cake. This was mainly reserved for the walled garden to be either dug into the vegetable beds as part of the four-course rotation or laid as a mulch on various permanent crops such as rhubarb, raspberries and hybrid berries or as a special treat for our extensive rose plantings. Sadly, we stopped in-house farming a few years ago, and that external supply dried up. It has been replaced by our own home-produced compost, which has proved to be just as good (well almost) as the manure.

'The nature and condition of your soil is one of the factors which will define the character of any garden, so it is a good idea to become familiar with its qualities and challenges as soon as possible.'

As always, having the appropriate facilities and
machinery ensure an efficient process.

*All other green waste
including grass clippings,
prunings, spent compost,
sweeper detritus, discarded
plant root balls (but excluding
noxious weeds) is composted
on a separate site to the wild
meadow heap. Again,
monthly turning will produce
a useable compost over a
twelve-month period.*

'Basically a compost heap is a slap-up meal for zillions of microorganisms that like nothing better than tucking into a twenty-course feast of green waste.'

I was a youthful fan of Lawrence D. Hills, the idiosyncratic but eminently practical founder of the Henry Doubleday Research Association (now Garden Organic), and as an idealistic young man I spent a happy and educative summer working on the HDRA's original Bocking trial ground. This left me well versed in the virtues, science and practice of successful composting, a background which has underpinned my entire horticultural career. All gardens generate green, compostable waste that can be converted into useful compost which can then be used as a soil conditioner, thus closing the nutrient and organic waste cycle and ensuring a healthy, fertile soil ad infinitum. However, to achieve this happy outcome you do need to invest some resources in creating an efficient area for it to take place.

Our system is simplicity itself. We have three composting areas, two in the grounds and one in the arboretum, each approximately 20 m/66 ft × 20 m in area. These are all hard surfaced, screened and divided into three. One is for woody material, one for the 'hay' generated off our extensive wildflower meadows, and one for dealing with all other green waste. In addition, the arboretum yard has a further area for the disposing of material that must not go into the compost cycle. These include noxious perennial weeds such as bindweed and creeping thistle, weeds laden with viable seed, diseased or pest-infested material, or any other material that may compromise the quality of the compost produced.

All woody material above 15 mm/five-eighths of an inch in diameter is kept separate and put through a chipper, which reduces it to a regular woodchip of approximately 15 mm dimensions. These are stockpiled to ultimately create a large pile up to 15 m/50 ft × 10 m/33 ft × 3 m/10 ft high and then left to mature for up to twelve months. After maturation it is used throughout the garden, principally as a moisture retaining, weed suppressing mulch.

All the 'hay' that comes off our extensive wildflower meadows is gathered into a large pile, and it is then turned every four to six weeks using a JCB, ideally even more regularly. This relatively frequent turning keeps the decomposition process active and ensures that within twelve months we have a useable compost with a consistency not dissimilar to chocolate ganache icing. Rich and moisture retentive, it is a little sticky to use neat so we generally incorporate it into existing soils in new developments.

Finally, all other green waste goes into another large heap. This is a mix of spent compost, old plants, lawn clippings, woody prunings of less than 15 mm diameter, leaves, road sweepings, the material from the big autumn tidy of the borders, and anything else that will decompose and is not noxious. This is allowed to accumulate over a twelve-month period and is 'pushed up' every couple of weeks to keep it tidy and help the decomposition process. After the last of the fallen leaves are cleared and the last borders cut back, normally around early March, we hire in a big industrial shredder for a day and the whole pile is shredded. This reduces it in bulk by about 40 per cent and instantly converts it into something closely resembling compost. A further maturation of a couple of months with one or two 'turns' produces a very useable, consistent and open soil conditioner that can serve as a mulch or be planted directly into, or blended through, existing soil.

Top: One of our three compost yards. St Andrew's Church in the background and the pile of green waste awaiting shredding behind the JCB.

Bottom: Because we have limited space, each year's compost production has to be used before the next year's can be shredded. All gardens of whatever size need to evolve an appropriate method for dealing with green waste.

COMPOST CORNER 2 – PRINCIPLES AND PRACTICE

As in all things, to become an effective composter it is important to understand a few scientific principles and absorb a few practical tips to achieve the desired end of 'green gold'. Principles first. Basically a compost heap is a slap-up meal for zillions of microorganisms that like nothing better than tucking into a twenty-course feast of green waste. The happy coincidental outcome of all their banqueting is a large pile of lovely compost rather than the usual post-party detritus. However, for the event to go with a swing the ambience and menu need to be right, so as a host you need to ensure the following:

~ plenty of organic matter in the right mix of materials and sizes – a well-balanced repast that will really get the guests gourmandizing;
~ air – the decomposers, who are the life and soul of the event, are aerobic: they can only function in the presence of oxygen;
~ moisture – who wants to go to a party and not have a tipple? No moisture equals no party. Equally an excess of drink turns the *bon vivants* into listless bores as the heap becomes anaerobic, producing slime rather than compost;
~ pH – too acid a diet results in a lack of appetite, so sometimes lime may need to be added to keep the guests consuming.

As with any good celebration, a great deal of heat is generated from the activities of the partygoers (the microorganisms). It is this 'exothermic reaction' which makes your heap steam in cold weather. Under ideal circumstances the temperature can rise to 70°C/158°F within the first seven days of making the heap, and at those temperatures the mix is pasteurized – killing all pests, diseases and weed seeds, hurrah!
Now for the practicalities in relation to the principles.

~ To achieve the appropriate mix of green waste that will provide the correct balance of nutrients, water and aeration for efficient compost production, you need to get the carbon/nitrogen ratio right. In practical terms this means combining roughly equal proportions of carbon-rich 'brown' materials – fibrous prunings, autumn leaves, old herbaceous stems – with nitrogen-rich 'green' materials: lawn mowings, kitchen waste, green leaves. This balance is not always easy to achieve, but if you are short of either type you can substitute a dose of nitrogen fertilizer for the missing 'green' component or a slurp of sawdust or cardboard for the 'brown'.
~ Even with the right mix, an uncovered heap can soon become saturated and anaerobic in wet weather. Water can always be added but not so easily removed, so covering a heap gives much better control of its moisture content.

~ In an ideal world a heap is made in one hit as this enables it to achieve a rapid build-up of microbial activity, therefore heat, therefore pasteurization. In reality this is rarely attainable. However, shredding 'brown' material before adding it to the pile helps to overcome this problem by reducing its size and increasing the surface area of the materials accessible to the microorganisms to work on, thus speeding up the decomposition process.

~ All other things being equal, the degree to which a stack heats up depends on the surface area to volume ratio. The smaller the heap, the greater the disproportion between those two and the less successful the process. Generally bigger is better.

~ The initial 'exothermic' period when you can really feel the heat soon cools down, principally because of reduced oxygen availability. In a similar fashion to stirring the embers of a dying fire and thus exposing unburnt fuel to additional oxygen, turning the heap reactivates it. By repeating this you can keep a pile active until it is fully decomposed.

It has been a long chapter but that is because at the end of the day the answer to good gardening really does lie in the soil.

'But the glory of the garden lies in more than meets the eye.
For where the old thick laurels grow, along the thin red wall,
You find the tool- and potting-sheds which are the heart of all;
The cold-frames and the hot-houses, the dung-pits and the tanks,
The rollers, carts and drain-pipes, with the barrows and the planks.'
Rudyard Kipling, 'The Glory of the Garden'

Infrastructure

John Sales, for many years Chief Gardens Adviser to the National Trust, always used to prefix any comment he made on gardens with the observation that 'a garden is a process and not a product', thus highlighting their dynamic and mutable character and the fact that they are only sustained by a constant and endless series of subtle interventions. Interventions carried out by gardeners who, like any other artist-craftsman, need an infrastructure to support their craft, whether that is the artist's studio, the furniture maker's workshop or Kipling's evocative list of the Victorian garden's life support system.

THE BACK SHEDS

Kipling, poet of empire and creator of 'Tommy Atkins', the unsung hero who sustained its imperial splendour, obviously had an equally realistic understanding of the nuts and bolts that underpinned the splendid edifice of the Victorian walled garden in its heyday. Whilst the owner would show off the pomp and splendour of his productive walled kingdom with its glittering glass palaces, hidden away – unseen and

Gardeners' Cottage, the traditional home of the Head Gardener, is immediately adjacent to the working heart of the garden, our yard.

127

unsung – on the horticulturally unproductive north-facing side of the 'thin red wall' lay a small hamlet of buildings and yards that housed the infrastructure needed to maintain the artifice of effortless perfection on display next door.

These would include fruit and flower rooms, a shed for trimming and washing vegetables before they went to the kitchen, and a room for packing the hampers which were sent up to the London residence at least once a week during the Season. There would also be fruit stores, stores for keeping root vegetables through the winter, and the warm, dark sheds where mushrooms were grown and seakale and rhubarb forced. Here too were the potting sheds, boiler room, Head Gardener's office, tool-sheds and possibly the bothy where the young gardeners lived. Close to the warmth of the boiler room and convenient for the glasshouses which needed attention last thing at night, the bothy could range from a rudimentary mess-room and sleeping quarters to a purpose-built house such as the impressive one at West Dean, built by the Jameses in 1896 in the north-west corner of the kitchen garden. The Head Gardener's own house, a substantial residence befitting his status, would also be built into or adjacent to the walled garden. In addition, the yards would harbour the more basic necessities of the kitchen garden: dung and compost heaps, garden refuse waiting to be burnt, barrels of liquid manure and soot water, loam heaps made from stacked turves, crock piles and mountains of pea sticks. As Kipling rightly observed, 'You find the tool- and potting-sheds which are the heart of all.'

....

A PLACE FOR EVERYTHING

Over a century later that need for a semi-invisible support structure to sustain the pageant of the garden remains just as vital as ever. At West Dean we have seven full-time gardeners, including myself and Sarah, plus a trainee and about forty volunteers and this workforce can only operate efficiently if they have the appropriate tools, materials and workspaces to carry out their tasks. Therefore, over the years a lot of time and effort has gone into ensuring that a suitable logistical underpinning is in place and is as well maintained as the garden itself. Some of this utilizes the earlier Victorian framework: the old garden stable converted to a charming small machinery store (hedge cutters, blowers, brush cutters, pedestrian mowers) or the old boiler house remodelled into an atmospheric potting shed where all of our extensive potting and repotting takes place. However, the bulk of it was installed new in the first ten years of the garden's redevelopment.

All too often one visits gardens where it seems to be assumed that the gardeners can operate effectively out of a couple of ramshackle sheds, and it is one of my proudest achievements that this is not the case at West Dean. The heart of our operation is the Gardens Yard, a tarmacked and properly drained area in the classic position on the north side of one of the east–west walls of the walled garden. Here we have a range of seven sheds, 4.5 m/15 ft wide and 5 m/16 ft deep, with large double doors and that are appropriately shelved out according to their respective functions.

I am a great believer in the old adage: 'a place for everything and

Top: In the foreground, on the north-facing wall of the kitchen garden, is the historic mushroom shed. The building in the opposite corner is the 'Bothy', purpose built as apprentice accommodation in the 1890s.

Bottom: Viewed from above, the array of walls, buildings and glasshouses within the walled garden does feel like a self-contained and purposeful community.

Following page: At the heart of the life of the garden is the garden's yard. Here are found the garden's mess-room, office, chemical store, machinery workshop, pot washing shed, potting shed and an extensive range of sheds for storage.

everything in its place'. This is a useful rule when you are the sole occupant of a site but absolutely essential when you have more than forty people using the same spaces and equipment. Time spent searching for things is frustrating and inefficient, and good housekeeping goes a long way to avoiding time wasting. Having said that, it takes constant vigilance on someone's part – mine in our case – to constantly reinforce the culture and pick up the pieces when the system breaks down. Perhaps the coda to the above should be: 'If in doubt turf it out.' In the same way that Parkinson's Law states that 'work expands to fill the time available,' so Buckland's law affirms that 'stuff accrues to fill the space available.' Every organization benefits from a regular therapeutic declutter.

To that end all of our materials are stored in as logical and transparent a fashion as possible and grouped according to function. The obvious example is the chemical store, where we have a statutory obligation to store the relatively limited range of herbicides and pesticides we use in a safe and compliant fashion. More attractively (it is a honeypot for photographers), the many thousands of terracotta pots we use have their own storage shed, where they are stacked according to size and type. And in the same vein we also have a dedicated pot-washing shed with three soaking sinks, five washing sinks, and extensive racks for drying washed pots, ready to be transferred back to the pot-shed for the next round of use. If that all sounds like a military operation, then at certain times of the year when two or three people are furiously scrubbing away it seems like an accurate description. Other sheds store fertilizers, rolls of netting and fleece, trestle tables (very useful temporary work stations), glass cloches, canes and stakes (also cleaned annually) plus general sundries. In addition, the walls of one are lined with large hooks from which are suspended dozens of loosely looped 25 m/80 ft coils of 10 mm/½ inch and 20 mm/¾ inch water hose and in front of which is a taxi rank of six liquid fertilizer dilutors, all kept filled with various feed formulations.

'As Kipling rightly observed, "You find the tool- and potting-sheds which are the heart of all." Over a century later, that need for a semi-invisible support structure to sustain the pageant of the garden remains a vital as ever.'

THE RIGHT TOOL

Adjacent to the hose-shed is the tool-shed. Here all of our hand tools are hung neatly in serried ranks by type from brooms through hoes to spades and shovels and all points between. We are not obsessive about their care, but one strict rule is that no tool goes back in the shed without being cleaned off in the wash-down tank outside the door. No one likes using someone else's grubby tool! And on a wet day we take the opportunity to sharpen hoes, shears and edging irons and to carry out any other running repairs required.

One of the pleasures of gardening is its physicality and immediacy, and this directness is reflected in the hand tools we use, which are little more than specialized extensions of the human anatomy. The essence of a good tool is that it should be simple, strong, easy to maintain and effective. Gadgets soon fall by the wayside, and most pieces in our tool-shed have hardly altered in centuries. The right tool, of good quality and well looked after, should last at least half a lifetime so buy the best you can. Cheap equals spades that bend as if caressed by Uri Geller and forks that

133

*With thousands of terracotta pots in use, pot washing
and storage is a high priority.*

spread more easily than the smoothest margarine. I have been buying the Bulldog Premier range for most of my working career, and short of driving over them with a tractor they seem to withstand all that daily professional use throws at them.

In the same range of buildings we have a 12 m/39 ft × 5 m/16 ft workshop with adequate lighting, ventilation and electrical supply and with work benches and tool boards, storage cupboards and racks around its outer edge, leaving a large central space capable of accommodating any larger machinery such as tractors or ride-on mowers that need to be repaired. This can also double as a decent work space for any other tasks that need to be undertaken from fabricating kilometres of steel path edging to painting machinery. And on the wall is the all-important whiteboard where any item brought into the workshop for repair is logged with date, 'donor' and perceived problem and is then returned to its proper home and removed from the board when repaired – very satisfying when it works!

SUPPORT SYSTEMS

Two other vital human spaces: the garden staff mess-room and the garden office. The former is home to the garden staff plus any volunteers who are on site on that day and can get a little snug on occasions. Like all such spaces it is homely rather than smart, but provides welcome dry and cosy break-time shelter on a cold winter's day. Vitally, it is cleaned at least once a week and has an annual purge to get rid of all the single gloves, torn waterproof trousers and other accumulated detritus that are magnetically drawn to its confines. It also enjoys the benefits of male and female toilets, a staff cloakroom and the heat exchanger room, which doubles as a drying room for wet clothing.

And the latter? Well, if the yard and associated sheds are the garden's engine room, then the office is its nerve centre: a 6 m/20 ft × 4 m/13 ft space whose interior we were fortunate to be able to completely redesign two decades ago. This gave us three work stations, lots of cupboard and shelf space, room for the now increasingly defunct filing cabinets, and plenty of walls on which to display an eclectic collection of garden memorabilia, posters, photos and related mementoes. It is a congenial room and is generally agreed by all who visit it to be both professional and *gemütlich*. Of course, twenty years ago we did not actually have computers, but we now have three: mine, Sarah's and a communal one for anyone who needs to use it, and like everybody else we are unable to function without them. From research to record keeping, communication to creativity, they are as essential to the smooth running of a large garden as good hand tools or decent machinery.

An equally vital addition to the modern professional gardener's armoury is the ubiquitous smartphone. Whether it is using the alarm function to remind you to turn off a sprinkler, the camera to record a particularly good plant combination, or simply to communicate with your staff scattered over the surrounding acres, it has become a lifeline.

All canes and stakes enjoy a minimum
of an annual clean and sort.

*Handwritten labels for use in the walled garden and the
'Green Goddess', the yard's green waste depository.*

PAINTING AND POLYTUNNELS

On a separate site about 50 m/160 ft away from the walled garden, we have a back-up area eponymously known as the agent's garden because historically it was the resident land agent's kitchen garden. We took it over more than twenty years ago, and terraced and regraded the sloping site to create level spaces for a growing area for raising plants, a machinery shed to store our fleet of seven mini tractors and ride-on mowers, and to erect three 4 m/13 ft × 12 m/39 ft polytunnels. These have proved enormously useful, although less as growing spaces – only one is generally used for this purpose – and more as additional storage space or for other tasks such as welding and more especially painting. With in excess of fifty items of garden furniture plus all of the 'lights' from the cold frames and pit houses, there is rarely a moment when some item is not being either sanded or painted, a hidden but vital element of the garden's maintenance schedule. On the same site and in a similar vein we also have a large wooden shed that acts as further storage space but is also set up for the year-round task of label painting. Our hundreds of wooden plant labels are an important element of both the ambience of the site and our commitment to visitor engagement. However, as each is rewritten every year, this is another of those ongoing maintenance cycles that doubles, along with pot washing, as an excellent wet weather job for those days when it is just too grim to be outside. In the same area we also have a space where each February we stockpile our mountain of hazel pea sticks and bean poles after we cut them in January. This is then drawn from through the growing season to provide sustainable and attractive plant supports in the borders and kitchen garden.

'I am a great believer in the old adage: "a place for everything and everything in its place." This is a useful rule when you are the sole occupant of a site but absolutely essential when you have more than forty people using the same spaces and equipment.'

ONE MAN'S WASTE IS . . .

Another vital, but often neglected, part of any large garden's organization is its green waste management system. Our process, and the three spaces in which it takes place, has been pretty fully covered in the previous chapter, but it is worth noting three items that facilitate the system's smooth running. Generally, large quantities of woody waste, say from felling a tree, are chipped *in situ* and transported to the chip pile from there – simple and straightforward. However, small amounts of woody waste are stockpiled in an area of the agent's garden until a sufficient quantity has accrued to justify setting up the chipper and trailer to deal with it, a significant saving of time and effort. Equally, some green waste – noxious weeds such as ground elder or bindweed, seed-laden weeds or diseased plants – cannot be put into the compost cycle. These are stockpiled on a concrete pad in the agent's garden and are ultimately disposed of in the service yard in St Roche's arboretum. And finally in the yard we have an old high-sided tipping trailer nicknamed the 'Green Goddess', after the old emergency fire engines. This is the receptacle for all of the small amounts of green waste generated daily from the walled garden and glasshouses; it is emptied when completely full, on average every six working days when properly filled.

*The machinery workshop is vital to the maintenance
of our extensive range of garden machinery.*

A regular and extensive repotting programme is essential
to maintain the glasshouse displays at the peak of perfection.
Christina potting aeoniums.

Below: We try to minimize the amount of irrigation we do but in times of drought a good range of easily accessible hose is essential. Dilutors for liquid feeding under glass in the foreground.

EAU DE VIE

Finally, one other vital element in any garden's life is a convenient supply of water, at reasonable pressure and accessible throughout the area. This was one of the first issues that we addressed by putting in a supply throughout the entire garden (excluding the wild garden) and arboretum. This was then supplemented by the installation of automated, pop-up irrigation systems in the high-profile turf areas around the house.

All infrastructure becomes invisible after installation, but despite this it remains the foundation on which the entire edifice of the garden is built. Whether you garden 100 sq m/1,075 sq ft or 40 hectares/ 100 acres, you ignore it at your peril.

EAU DE VIE

'Who loves a garden, loves a greenhouse too
Unconscious of a less propitious clime,
There blooms exotic beauty, warm and snug
While the winds whistle and the snows descend.
The spiry myrtle with unwithering leaf
Shines there and flourishes.'
William Cowper

Under glass

The steamy heat of house 10 supports an eclectic selection of exotic plants whose bold foliage creates a truly jungle atmosphere as they mature. Nepenthes, Codiaeum, Begonia, Anthurium and palms all add to the show.

Cowper was right! Languishing in the steamy heat of a lushly vegetated glasshouse whilst winter rages outside is both deeply comforting and the ultimate expression of the gardener's desire to mould our intransigent climate to their own growing ends. This quest for the perfect artificial environment in which to grow the exotic and unseasonable can be traced from Roman 'stoves' to eighteenth-century orangeries, but it was not until the 1840s that the technology finally caught up with the gardener's ever-expanding ambition. The two major limiting factors were a suitable supply of light and heat. The former was solved by the development of sheet glass and the repeal of the punitive Glass Tax in 1845, and the latter by the development of efficient hot water heating systems. These, plus cheap coal, mass production of cast iron glasshouse and heating parts, an enormous influx of horticultural exotica from around the empire, and the fashion for vast bedding schemes using huge quantities of half-hardy annuals, paved the way for the glasshouse to move centre stage in the high Victorian garden.

CRYSTAL PALACES

For the next seventy-five years an extensive glasshouse range was at the heart of any self-respecting large Victorian or Edwardian garden. These were of two types. First, the conservatory, generally a palatial glass extension of the living space of the great house where the cream of the floral crop was conveniently and sumptuously displayed for the pleasure of the family and their guests. And, second, the glasshouse range, normally located at some distance from the house within the protective surrounds of the walled garden. This was the backstage that supported the theatre of both conservatory and house and where, in addition to this floral performance, a diverse range of high-quality fruit and vegetables for the kitchen and table were also produced.

These immense glasshouse ranges – the orchard house at Drumlanrig in Scotland was 152 m/500 ft long, 5.5 m/18 ft wide and had 915 m/3,000 ft of heating pipes and a mini rail track down its length – were masterpieces of industrial design and mechanical engineering. Within them the head gardener and his glasshouse foreman and staff were able to demonstrate their knowledge and skill by growing to perfection a huge variety of plants ranging from figs to ferns, peaches to palms, and oranges to orchids in a year-round tour de force of matchless horticultural wizardry. But those glory days were numbered, and with the huge social and economic upheavals engendered by the two world wars they slid inexorably into decline and dereliction.

Top: The old hot bed frame that would have relied on fermenting manure to supply its heat source in the nineteenth century was, along with the rest of the glasshouse range, in very poor condition in 1991.

Bottom: Over a two-year period the entire range was restored to its late nineteenth-century glory. The external trench where historically the fermenting manure would have been placed is very obvious in its cleared-out state after restoration.

A STAR IS BORN

And this was the situation when we arrived at West Dean in 1991, to find an impressive, albeit derelict, collection of Victorian glass that had been neglected for the last forty years. The majority of the buildings were manufactured by Foster and Pearson of Beeston in Nottinghamshire (the Rolls-Royce of glasshouse construction) during the period 1891–1900, and we still have the original contract documents from their purchase. Their survival through to the present day, despite decades of neglect, was nothing short of miraculous and amply demonstrated the quality of materials (mainly Archangel pine and cast iron), design and craftsmanship involved in their fabrication.

Sadly by the 1990s the vast majority of these once nationally ubiquitous glasshouse ranges had been demolished. This meant that given the quantity (thirteen glasshouses, three cold frames and a hotbed frame), quality and period homogeneity of the West Dean range, they offered a unique opportunity to revitalize at least one representative example of our nineteenth-century glasshouse heritage for future generations to enjoy. As a consequence, this became the centrepiece of our whole garden renovation plan. The aim of the restoration was to retain the buildings' historic character whilst enabling their full horticultural use with only a minimal staff, roughly one and a half people, compared with the six gardeners who tended them in their prime. To that end a new, fully automated heating system was installed, and electric

'The aim of the restoration was to retain the buildings' historic character whilst enabling their full horticultural use with only a minimal staff, roughly one and a half people.'

Far left, top: Houses 1–3 prior to restoration. Minus glass and strangled by encroaching vegetation, their future looked bleak.

Far left, bottom: After much hard labour a miraculous transformation was wrought and the whole area took on a purposeful and disciplined air that reflected its nineteenth-century character.

Left, top: Recycling of materials was a big part of the project. These tiles had originally been part of the Orangery floor. Past bricklaying skills were to prove very useful.

Bottom: It is now twenty-five years since the walled garden and glasshouses were originally restored and few will remember the scenes of dereliction prior to that. As with all aspects of gardening the secret of long-term success is a consistent and constant maintenance programme.

pumps were fitted to allow us to use the copious amounts of free, soft rainwater collected off the glasshouses and stored in huge subterranean tanks alongside them. However, all venting and watering are still done by hand, a very demanding and time-consuming activity in the growing season.

The actual restoration was carried out in-house, with the gardeners clearing the mantle of rampant vegetation and accumulated debris and our building team carrying out the structural makeover. Astonishingly, given their parlous appearance and decades of neglect, most of the timber was still sound, and after a vigorous sanding down and replacement of any failed wood, they were ready for the first of many coats of paint. As nearly all of the glass had long since disappeared, a completely new set was installed, carefully ensuring that they all had the requisite 'beaver tail', a shallow curve, on their bottom edge. This is a traditional glasshouse glazier's trick that ensures water runs down the centre of the glass pane and not the rot-susceptible glazing bars, as would happen with a straight bottom edge: eminently practical and pleasingly attractive. The transformation from derelict skeletons to dazzling beauties was rapid and dramatic, and wandering through their pristine cathedral-like interiors it seemed almost sacrilegious to clutter their clean lines with rambunctious vegetation. However, that moment soon passed and the task of repopulating their empty spaces began.

Fortunately we had records of the original growing regimes, and today's management is generally modelled on these but adjusted to accommodate our very different circumstances. These changes generally relate to lower staffing levels and the transition from a private garden for one family's gratification to a public garden with over 70,000 visitors a year. In the past the glasshouse display was transported to the house for its audience of family and guests to enjoy, whereas now it remains *in situ* and its audience of visitors comes to it. This is effectively a complete reversal of function and nicely illustrates how the contemporary walled garden has been transformed from a lowly back-up area to being the jewel in the crown of the visitors' experience.

FRUIT UNDER GLASS

The glasshouses are numbered 1 to 26, representing the number of separate compartments within the thirteen houses. This offers twenty-six potentially different growing environments, a facility that was, and still is, integral to the diversity of crops grown. Broadly speaking, we have six fruit houses, eight floral display houses, ten multi-purpose houses (either vegetable growing or plant production, depending on the season) and two specialist propagation houses. In addition, there is a vegetable growing frame and three production frames for growing on and hardening off potted plants.

The fruit houses are all on south-facing walls and are three-quarter span houses, the classic design for growing fruit under glass. Their position and configuration ensure maximum light and heat penetration, with the large back wall storing radiant heat during the day and releasing it overnight, plus excellent ventilation and air circulation to help reduce

151

*The 100-year-old fig responded well to its original
'pudding bowl' trim twenty-five years ago but finally succumbed
to old age and has now been replaced.*

....

'Every winter, over a two-month period, four members of staff systematically clean each of the houses from top to bottom. This involves removing all plants that are movable, hand scrubbing the framework, cleaning the glass and then disinfecting the entire space.'

fungal problems. We have two fig houses where the figs are grown in brick 'boxes' to restrict their root run and, in theory, temper their tendency to produce rampant vegetative growth at the expense of fruiting. The two original, 100-year-old specimens were completely feral when we arrived and had long outgrown their houses; they were given a 'kill or cure' haircut reducing them to a 1 m/39 inch stump. As is so often the case in these situations, they responded with alacrity and had soon been trained out as fans to once again cover their supporting wire framework and produce delicious crops of luscious Brown Turkey figs. However, over the last two decades they had declined, and when their respective houses were recently renovated we took the opportunity to remove them and replace them with vigorous new plants, thus starting the cycle again for the next century. Professional gardeners tend to be a pretty unsentimental lot.

In the past considerable glasshouse space was dedicated to dessert grape production, and we still have three active vineries. The grapes are grown on a rod and spur system, and have a high labour demand in the first half of the year when the new growth needs regular pruning and tying in. This is then followed by the painstaking thinning of the selected fruit bunches, when up to 70 per cent of the grapes are removed to allow the remainder to swell to their optimum size, a job demanding patience and a strong neck. We also have a number of standard vines in pots, a favourite Victorian conversation piece when they were taken to the dining table so that guests could select their own bunch direct from the vine.

One house is dedicated to peach and nectarine production, and this has an interesting curved framework that allows twice the number of trees to be grown in the space as the curve allows sunlight to penetrate to the trees grown on the rear wall as well as those on the curved framework. They are grown as fans on a replacement system: having established a permanent framework, the fruit is actually produced on the previous season's branches, which then have to be replaced each year by cutting out the fruited wood and tying in the young current season's branches. This is another skilled and time-consuming job as each full-size fan, of which there are eight, takes four to six hours to complete. But it is a task made well worthwhile when you bite into a perfectly ripe peach and nearly drown in the juices!

Equally flavoursome is the crop of early pot-grown strawberries that are to be found on their dedicated shelf. These are bought in as cold-stored plants in January, potted up and started into life in a warm greenhouse, and then moved to their fruiting position by late April. They are an early delight and, judging by the number of 'strawberry' boards to be found throughout the glasshouse range, must have been as popular with our forebears as they are with us.

....

FLOWERS TO FRAMES

The floral display houses are primarily venues for a range of diverse semi-permanent, themed collections that, whilst remaining fundamentally the same over the years, also undergo subtle evolution to maintain interest. Broadly speaking, they are made up of tropical and temperate floral and foliage display collections, including orchids, which are housed in

The winter glasshouse clean up requires a lot
of elbow grease, copious buckets of hot, soapy water
and a sense of humour!

All of the fruit houses have an extensive wire support system on which to grow the fruit. Periodically this needs retensioning.

free-standing 'span' houses that are capable of sustaining appropriate overnight temperatures in the winter months. In contrast, there are other collections, principally of ferns, fuchsias and geraniums, that thrive in the cooler and shadier conditions to be found in the two lean-to houses on one of the north-facing walls of the walled garden. All of these collections need to be actively managed in a rolling annual programme of repropagation and potting on, plus the ceaseless daily round of watering, liquid feeding, removing dead foliage and flowers, and pest and disease control, the last now primarily delivered using biological controls. The final category of glasshouse function alternates between plant production, vegetable production and overwintering half-hardy specimens, depending on the time of year. However, the two 'pit' houses, the once very popular semi-sunken glasshouses roofed with English Lights, plus the old cucumber and melon houses play a particularly important part in this cropping merry-go-round.

Every winter, over a two-month period, four members of staff systematically clean each of the houses from top to bottom. This involves removing all plants that are movable, hand scrubbing the framework, cleaning the glass and then disinfecting the entire space. This is a gruelling but vital task that is fundamental both to the presentation and preservation of the buildings and also to the hygiene of their growing environments. Thus, at some point all of the houses are overwintering elements of the permanent collection. In late winter the collections return to their normal homes, and the current season's new plants for both glasshouse and outdoor display are potted up and grown on, ready to be moved to their final homes through the spring. Once these have gone, the spaces that they have vacated are filled by those vegetable crops grown under glass through the summer, such as tomatoes, aubergines and chillies, and so the cycle closes.

This leaves the small but very important house 7 and 8. This is unusual in that it was the only one commissioned by Edward and not Willy James, was erected in the 1970s and not the 1890s, and although timber framed was built by C. H. Whitehouse and not Foster and Pearson. Here the bulk of our propagation takes place, a process aided by its heated and closed benches, its relatively small size, and the fact that every winter we line it with insulating bubble plastic to enable us to achieve the high ambient temperatures required for the propagation programme.

Finally we have the cold frames. These were an important adjunct to the main range of glasshouses in the nineteenth-century walled garden, providing additional but cheaper protected growing environments for everything from forcing bulbs and starting seedlings to hardening off nursery stock before planting out in the garden, exactly as they are used today.

TRIAL BY GLASS

Gardening under glass is like gardening on amphetamines – everything happens faster, more dramatically and more catastrophically – and to use and maintain such a complex and diverse range successfully over decades requires a high degree of technical knowledge, organizational ability,

159

House 7-8 is used for propagation. Here semi-ripe cuttings
and seed sowings are started off before being moved to
other houses to be grown on.

The closed case has a thermal blanket on its bench
that supplies a gentle bottom heat to assist germination
of seeds or rooting of cuttings.

We call house 9 our temperate display house where a wide range of both flowering and foliage plants are carefully staged to show them off to best effect. Achimenes, Kohleria *and* Impatiens *are the principal floral components of the display pictured here.*

creative talent and sheer doggedness. Unsurprisingly, it is not for everyone and is the principal reason why very often a well-run garden is let down by its glasshouse facilities. Over the years we have inducted a number of horticultural trainees and staff into the mysteries of this most demanding art, and it is fair to say that it is the most challenging exercise they undertake. The benefit that makes a glasshouse so desirable – complete control of the environment – is also the factor that makes it so demanding, because you as the controller have to ensure that all of the inputs (water, nutrition, sunlight, temperature and pest and disease control) are appropriately managed to create the correct environment for your charges. This is hard enough in a fully automated, digitally controlled twenty-first-century commercial glasshouse growing a monoculture of poinsettias, but exponentially more demanding in a Victorian range growing a bewilderingly diverse range of plants with very different individual requirements and whose well-being is down to the experience, judgement and actions of one individual.

Inevitably, plenty of mistakes are made and a few plant casualties fall by the wayside, but generally after a year people are beginning to get the hang of it. And what is the 'it' they have to get the hang of? First, it is a finely tuned awareness of, and sensitivity to, the ever changing growing environment. Second, the capacity to interpret the message that the morphology and appearance of each plant type send to the gardener regarding its likely growing requirements. And, third, the ability to respond to these two stimuli with appropriate management decisions about watering, venting and nutrition. It is this steep learning curve that hones the rough diamond of the apprentice gardener into the polished stone of a true glasshouse gardener, an individual at the apogee of their craft.

Lawns

This area was tightly mown grass all year round until a decade ago. By simply altering the mowing regime we now enjoy floral colour climaxing with this blaze of buttercups.

Every three or four years Sarah and I head south to Australia to catch up with friends and family in Victoria. As the plane climbs away from Gatwick, the Home Counties are laid out below us in all their verdant grassiness, a tourist board tapestry that fully justifies the description of 'green and pleasant land'. After nineteen hours or so, the plane is cruising over the great red centre of Australia, a rocky desert landscape as far removed from Sussex as can be imagined. One familiar, lush and green, and the other dry, dusty but sprinkled with its own unique and tough vegetation neatly adapted to the extreme conditions in which it grows. And the point of that tale? Well, when Kipling began his poem 'Our England is a garden', he might more accurately have written 'Our England is a lawn' because no other country in the world has such an innate capacity to grow turf with such consummate ease. Economically it was the rich grassy pastures of medieval England that made the country wealthy on the back of the wool trade, and culturally it is the luxuriant sweeping lawns of *le jardin anglais* that turn our overseas gardening admirers green with sward envy. We are a nation defined by our herbage as much as our heritage!

THE LAWN AS LUNG

Given the natural advantages we enjoy, it is hardly surprising that the lawn has been a constant of our garden history and that we have elevated its cultivation to that of an art form. But is its relative ease of cultivation in Britain sufficient reason to explain its dominance in our gardens? Well, yes, partially. Up to a point anyone who is capable of pushing a mower is capable of keeping their garden presentable. Thus, when you take a train into London you look down on a plethora of back gardens that are effectively green deserts. Devoid of beauty and sensual stimulation and scalped within an inch of their lives – but green and neat, ergo job done. However, beyond the sward as ecological manifest destiny or the garden as battlefield, there are lots of positive design and functional reasons for the presence of lawns in almost all gardens in the kingdom. With their uniformity and smoothness they act as the perfect foil for the vegetative structural and textural excitement that arises around them. If the plants are the furnishings of the garden, then the lawn creates the room in which they are displayed.

Equally, as a user-friendly means of surfacing large areas of outdoor space for recreation and leisure, grass has no equal. Compare the grim experience of traversing a stark supermarket car park on a hot summer's day with strolling on a cool and caressing grass sward under shady groves. Hell and heaven incarnate. It comes as no surprise to me that many people make great claims for the therapeutic benefits of a barefoot, meditative meander over dew-speckled grass. Apparently it releases negative ions, but at the very least it is amazingly soothing. In a different vein, despite the technological improvements in artificial turf, no clubs in the Football League play on it, and domestically its use is pretty well restricted to harsh urban sites where grass would not survive. Yes, grass remains central to our national self-image, and despite frequent predictions of the lawn's demise, I suspect it will remain integral to the majority of gardens for the foreseeable future.

However, that does not mean we need to remain wedded to the mower and the sprayer. West Dean provides an excellent example of how changes in the way the turf is managed open up a plethora of possibilities for using swards to create a wealth of different gardening experiences. When we arrived at West Dean every piece of grass was mowed as regularly and trimly as possible, with the seeming aspiration to convert the bulk of the garden to a bowling green. Bizarrely this also included the arboretum, where the then 'warden' spent most of the summer enacting a grassy version of the myth of Sisyphus. Whilst this had the merit of looking neat and tidy and left no one in any doubt that the place was being managed, it was visually monotonous, sensually sterile and a completely inappropriate and wasteful use of resources.

EDGE CREEP

Alongside this mowing madness we had a classic case of 'edge creep'. Extensive lawns have extensive edges, and unless defined by some permanent material they inevitably retreat from their original line. Where this was originally alongside a hard surface, say tarmac, the end

'When Kipling wrote, "Our England is a garden", he might more accurately have written "Our England is a lawn". We are a nation defined by our herbage as much as our heritage!'

*Navigating around the trained fruit circles is
quite demanding but the crisply mown grass sets
them off to perfection.*

*The contrast between neatly mown turf and the
central wildflower swards is one of the defining features
of the fruit garden.*

The efficient management of the wildflower swards
is only possible with appropriate equipment, in this case
an Amazone Groundkeeper flail mower and a system
to deal with the arisings.

result is miles of mini trench systems created by the over-enthusiastic use of the edging iron, a particularly male affliction. This is both ugly and a maintenance nightmare, eats up hours of pointless effort and, once you start looking, is an ubiquitous blight on most gardens. My gardening career thus far had cynically taught me that getting the mowing and edging right was the narrow gate through which you gained access to the approbation and therefore support of your superiors. All the floristic fireworks in the world did not pack the respectful punch garnered from a crisp drive edge and a well-mown lawn: achieve these and the rest would follow. As a consequence, we started a rolling programme of redefining all existing edges and kept that up over the next two decades to bring us to our current state of edging nirvana where every margin in the garden – be it border, path or drive – is set in metal (and occasionally stone).

This has a number of positive impacts, all of which are equally applicable in the domestic garden:

~ No more edge creep and therefore a farewell to mini Western Front trench systems snaking around the garden.
~ All edges are efficiently and easily maintained, giving a crisp finish to the garden and re-energizing the staff, who can now redirect their efforts to more creative projects.
~ Improved output and outcomes from mowing, as it is easier and more effective to mow a well-defined and supported edge.

'Having established a programme of high-quality lawns, we felt empowered to take a walk on the wild side in other areas. If you are to take people with you in this process, they need to feel it is a conscious decision and not just a decline in standards.'

EDGE CORSETS

Our method of tackling the problem was to design and make our own metal edging. This had the virtue of being cheap, simple to fabricate and install and, despite making a huge positive impact on the appearance and ambience of the garden overall, is almost invisible in itself.

Our methodology was refined over the years but broadly consisted of taking a 6m/20ft-long strip of 7.5 cm/3 inch × 5 mm/¼ inch mild steel flat and welding 23cm/9inch-long legs in 25 mm/1 inch × 25 mm × 5 mm mild steel angle iron at 50 cm/20 inch intervals along its length. These were set 10 mm/½ inch below the top of the edge to remove any likelihood of it being caught by mowers. In addition, a 12cm-/5inch-long 'fish plate' cut out of the steel flat was welded to project 6 cm/2½ inches beyond one end of the steel flat. This was to enable joining the lengths. Initially we painted the lengths, but as this took more time than the actual fabrication and failed after a few years, we soon converted to installing untreated sections, which proved cheaper and perfectly acceptable. Equally we initially drilled and bolted the sections, which proved awkward and prone to failure, resulting in the adoption of welding the sections together. Finally we have adjusted the 'weight' of the steel used to suit specific conditions: heavier in heavily trafficked areas, lighter where tighter bends were needed, such as circles around tree bases. The heavier the gauge, the higher the price, the harder to bend.

Installation is simplicity itself. The course of the line is marked using aerosol road marking paint, the line cut out if necessary, the metal edge 'offered up' to it, the leg positions marked on the soil and 'drilled' with a

The last stage of our protracted edging campaign
has been to permanently metal edge all grass/border
interfaces with our homemade edging system.

This area above the pergola was originally a lawn tennis court. For the last twenty years it has been the home of the West Dean Bowls Club, who have taken on responsibility for the demanding maintenance schedule required to keep such an exacting sports surface in fine mettle.

substantial fencing bar, and then the whole piece tapped into position by two sledge-hammer-wielding operatives. Once a decent run is installed, it is welded *in situ* and any regrading/backfilling with soil takes place. Not subtle but effective and fast. It is worth noting that proprietary brands of edging material are now available although they do not look as robust as ours.

SWARD ALTERNATIVES

Having started the process of getting some clarity back into the edging of the garden, we felt that the time was right to reorder the mowing regime rather than maintain a simple 'one scalp trims all' approach. The aim was to take the monoculture we had inherited and diversify it to offer a multitude of experiences and functions that would achieve a number of objectives:

~ To use differential mowing to help define the nebulous expanses
   of featureless lawn that made up a substantial portion of the garden.
~ To create subliminal circulation patterns that would enhance the
   visitors' movement through the site.
~ To develop the floristic content of these areas by the introduction
   of new species by a variety of methods.
~ To extend the season of floral interest by extensive naturalization
   of bulbs in the newly created meadow areas.
~ To add a whole new layer of textural interest to the grounds via
   the existing herbage in its juvenile, mature and harvested phases.

First, we had to decide where we wanted to retain traditional, high-quality lawns with their manicured, lush surfaces redolent of status and privilege. Logically these were immediately around the house, the Visitor Centre, the sunken garden, the terraces and two small areas of recreational turf, the bowling green and croquet lawn. Such a baize-like appearance can only be achieved with a high commitment of resources, the first of which was the installation of an automatic watering system. Having worked in Australia where such systems are de rigueur in high-end landscapes, I knew this was an investment that, despite being totally superfluous in wet summers, would enable us to water effectively and efficiently in dry ones. In addition, a programme of fertilization, weed control, scarification and, most importantly, a regular – ideally twice a week – mow with a well-set cylinder mower rapidly brought these lawns up to par.

A WALK ON THE WILD SIDE

Having established that we were capable of and committed to a programme of high-quality lawn care, we felt empowered to take a walk on the wild side in other areas. And this is an important practical point. If you are to take people with you in this process of adopting a more relaxed style of presentation, they need to feel that it is a conscious

Top: In mid-May large tracts of meadow are illuminated by the unfeasibly golden glow of sheets of buttercups. A nightmare in agricultural pasture but in our meadows they are a simple, spirit-lifting joy.

Bottom: The statuesque spikes of foxgloves echo the birch trunks behind and complement the star burst ox-eye daisies in the foreground, St Roche's arboretum.

*Over half a million bulbs have been naturalized
using this basic but effective system. The results give
great pleasure from January to June.*

management choice and not simply a decline in standards. The juxtaposition of highly managed turf with the unbuttoned exuberance of a midsummer meadow reassures the more faint-hearted that herbal anarchy has not been loosed upon the world, and they can then enjoy both experiences for their different qualities.

Generally our starting point was to define the area to be converted with the ubiquitous hoses and aerosol paint, then simply stop mowing and see what happened. Mostly what happened ranged from underwhelming but unthreatening to spectacular and immediately life-enhancing with very few disasters in between. This 'suck it and see' approach is simplicity itself (just stop mowing), costs nothing, and should the outcome be totally abhorrent is instantly reversible (just start mowing again). Having lived with an area for a summer, we would feel confident as to its future potential and be aware of any nascent problems; based on that we would decide whether to continue next year, retrench or expand. I cannot think of one area that, having been given the meadow treatment, was subsequently returned to a regular mowing regime. The reality has been that the programme has been resolutely expansionist, and my estimate would be that approximately 60 per cent of the mowable area within the garden is now given over to meadow, quite a turnaround from the parade ground approach of yesteryear.

FLORAL FIRE POWER

Most of the converted areas were not a riot of floristic diversity, so the next stage was to enhance the offer. This was achieved by three principal means.

~   First, the introduction of bulbs. Because of the expansive and rural nature of the site and a desire for a more natural effect, these have been kept to a relatively restricted palette and with a bias to the smaller, less gaudy varieties. The aim has been to create spectacular but subtle displays that feel felicitous and uncontrived, not always easy to pull off. To achieve that goal all of the naturalized bulbs (in excess of 500,000) have been planted individually, by hand and by a team of three or four, depending on the size of bulb. The first step is an individual wielding a fencing bar with which to make the holes. This is the critical position as aesthetically they determine the pattern of distribution (and therefore its 'naturalness') and also set the working pace (and therefore productivity). I have always chosen to occupy that role and have Charles Atlas-like biceps as a consequence! Then comes the planter, who places the bulb down the hole, easy with small ones like crocus but more problematic with the bigger narcissi: hence the need for two on occasions. And finally the hole closer, an operation achieved by a well-aimed side blow with a club hammer to the top of the hole. Simple but surprisingly effective, allowing us to plant up to 8,000 bulbs a day depending on bulb size and soil type, and the method by which every bulb has been planted. Of course, this first planting is only an initial investment in the Bank of Beauty that in years to come will pay a handsome dividend in the ever-increasing display generated by self-propagation by both seed and offsets.

181

*Fresh tree foliage, buttercups
and ox-eye daisies: England
in May!*

~ Second, by growing select subjects as plugs and then planting them into the area. In the early days we collected large amounts of seed from nearby populations of primroses and cowslips, both locally common, and grew them on as plugs in tens of thousands. These were then planted in the same way as the bulbs and with the same net effect of accruing compound floral interest, so that now both the gardens and arboretum are generously splashed with the delicate yellow of these two favourites of mine. Other less vigorous subjects have also been given the same treatment, but bearing in mind the amount of work required our favoured option is the next in the list.

~ Overseeding can be very effective with more vigorous subjects and with less dense swards. Unlike twenty-five years ago, there are now a number of reputable suppliers of wildflower seed from whom large quantities can be purchased. We have had great success introducing things like yellow rattle, ox-eye daisy and meadow cranesbill by overseeding, and it is cheap and effective. Our method is to scalp the sward to be seeded and then open it up even more by scarifying and removing the arisings. The seed is then bulked up at least sixfold by mixing it through with dry, fine sand, scattered evenly by hand in at least two different directions, and then rolled with a heavy roller to ensure good contact between seed and soil. We generally do this around early October when the grass is slowing down and there is plenty of heat and moisture in the ground to encourage rapid germination.

MEADOWS FROM A PACKET

We have also created a number of meadows from scratch by seed. The most important factor in this process is to start with as weed-free a seedbed as possible. To achieve this we spray the area with glysophate in early spring, cultivate it and then spray any new vegetation that emerges. This process is repeated throughout the summer and then the wildflower seed sown, as above, in the early autumn. In very dock-infested areas we have actually extended this to a two-year fallow period. Once the meadow has germinated and is growing, weed control can only be by time-consuming and tiring spot spraying so, as always, it pays to be patient in your preparation.

Whatever the method of achieving the goal, the combination of well-tended turf contrasted with the floristically and texturally ebullient meadows is now a signature dish of the West Dean menu.

'The best time to plant a tree was twenty years ago.
The next best time is now.'
Chinese proverb

Trees

*Ornamental tree planting
in the garden and park
and forestry planting in
the background; whether
individual or massed, trees
define West Dean.*

For most people, planting a tree is the most significant deed they will
perform in their gardening lives. It is an act of horticultural faith in the
future, offering an inheritance that usually only comes to full fruition
generations hence. The small specimen they place in the ground may
outlive them by centuries, massively outgrow them in stature, and
ultimately dominate its landscape and modify its environment in a fashion
almost unimaginable to its long composted foster parent. And, like
parenthood, the planting of trees is not something to enter into lightly.
The responsibilities are many, the pitfalls plentiful and the outcome
uncertain, but a world without trees would be as unimaginable and as
sterile as a world without children. They are our future.

Try visualizing a world without trees. Not easy is it? Some friends of
ours recently announced their retirement from leafy Sussex to the windswept Orkneys. Having shown us a selection of images of sandy, empty
beaches, dramatic unpeopled bays and rolling moorland, my immediate
reaction was: 'Where are the trees?' That experience proved a couple of
things to me.

~   A landscape does not have to have trees in it to be beautiful.
    Orkney is.

187

*Trees are long-term investments. Buy the best stock
you can and plant it properly: at the right depth,
well firmed in and kept weed free.*

Formative pruning at the outset will ensure you
efficiently achieve your planting objectives and save
a lot of work in the future.

Top: This horse chestnut was planted to replace one lost in the 1997 storm. Sadly, horse chestnuts are now under increasing stress from canker and leaf miner attack and there is a question mark over their long-term viability.

Bottom: A Cornus kousa in full flower in St Roche's arboretum. A mix of trees of different stature achieves that variety of canopy layering that makes for attractive arboreta.

~ A landscape with trees is infinitely more visually and ecologically diverse, textured and multilayered than one without.

~ I probably should not move to Orkney (despite its many other attractions).

SAVANNA DREAMING

I am no anthropologist, but the theory that much of the design of our garden spaces is an atavistic re-creation of the savannas of our early hominid ancestors in East Africa seems quite plausible. Savannas are a mixed woodland/grassland ecosystem that cover about 20 per cent of the earth's surface and are frequently found in the transitional zone between rainforest and desert or grassland. They are distinguished by having trees being sufficiently widely spaced to prevent canopy closure. This open canopy allows enough light to reach the ground to support an unbroken herbaceous layer, generally grass. Their formation is characterized by a seasonal water supply – generally confined to one wet season – and by the occurrence of regular dry season wildfires. The latter phenomenon is often exaggerated by anthropogenic fire: the use of fire by humans as a management tool to regenerate the herbaceous layer without destroying the tree cover.

The argument is that despite humanity having long since scattered around the globe and adapted to the plethora of different ecosystems found over its surface, we still carry within our collective unconscious a sense of the rightness of that landscape type as a space to inhabit: a prelapsarian Eden that we are programmed to re-create wherever we find ourselves. Now obviously the UK is not a region noted for its extensive savannas, but the evolution of wood pasture through the manipulation of the tree canopy and grassland by controlled grazing of deer or cattle has produced that quintessentially English topographic feature, the landscape or deer park, adding yet another layer of cultural conditioning to our love affair with this scenic archetype.

Whatever the origins, the reality is that we feel most comfortable in a mosaic of human-scaled spaces that alternate a sense of enclosure with the opening up of expansive spaces and framed views whilst also generating orchestrated contrasts of light and dark, warm and cool, sun and shade, mystery and revelation. And none of that is possible without the scale and vertical dimension of trees and their ability to multilayer space from ground level to lofty heights through the complex tracery of their branch patterns.

THE TREE AS STAGE SET

It is my great good fortune to live and work in a place that is blessed with an extensive and diverse population of trees. About one-third of West Dean's 2,400 hectares/6,000 acres is given over to forestry, a tapestry of native hardwoods and exotic conifer plantations. Primarily they are managed commercially with the aim of maximizing the return on the

191

'The highest accolade one can receive after carrying out such pruning is silence, because when it is skilfully implemented no one realizes that you have done it: not a task for egotists!'

investment, an investment that operates in generations rather than years or even decades! However, a very important secondary function is their contribution to the landscape of the area with its mix of majestic mature beech stands, younger woodlands being developed by natural regeneration, and densely populated conifer plantations all adding mass and vertical contrast to the mosaic of pasture, arable fields and hedgerows that comprise the remaining 1,620 hectares/4,000 acres. Within the designed landscape of the gardens, landscape park and arboretum, the emphasis shifts from commercial value to design value. This is most evident if you stand at the front door of the house and look south. The tree planting within the gardens is designed to frame that view by enclosing it to east and west. Then, in the middle distance, the unencumbered sweep of the park is punctuated and articulated by a series of individual specimen trees and clumps until, finally, the outer edges of the park are encompassed by a series of woodland plantations that contain the view and force the eye to rest on the exquisite scene laid before it. Obviously, this is landscaping of a herculean order, and the primary function of the trees in this situation is to provide building blocks of framing mass at a scale appropriate to the landscape of which they are a part. Generally, they are not read as individuals nor are the idiosyncrasies of their individual branch frameworks significant in themselves

However, as you move through the gardens, the scale becomes more intimate and the trees once more become individuals whose specific structural characteristics become significant, both in themselves and also in their relationship with other trees and plants. In the UK, with its almost unparalleled ability to grow half-decent turf without too much effort, the most common means of creating glade-like spaces is to have a lawn or, less commonly, an area of low-growing herbaceous planting of a very limited species mix. The enclosure is created by the triple tiers of taller herbaceous planting, shrubs and understorey trees, and finally the canopy trees.

CROWN LIFTING AND CREATIVE PRUNING

One of the problems inherent in the shrub and tree components of any design is that they progressively lose their clarity of structure and spatial organization as they mature. Without careful editing the desired layering of vegetation, the coherence of definition between different plant types, and the interplay of open and closed vegetation can easily be lost as everything grows into everything else in the battle for light and resources. Left unmanaged, all of these once separate layers tend to merge into one dense thicket that is blurred, closed and unapproachable and from which the original visual diversity is lost. To prevent this happening regular interventions are necessary, ideally from the inception.

This is an aspect of the management of the gardens at West Dean I particularly enjoy and, as a consequence, one I pay careful attention to. Trees may require pruning for various reasons – safety, restriction in size, remedial action after wind damage – but the bulk of our pruning is what I call 'creative' in that it is about enhancing the tree's aesthetic impact

With maturity the fruit trees trained as
'four-winged pyramids' and 'goblets' have become
a major feature of the walled garden.

either in itself or in relation to surrounding vegetation. I have always loved pruning and training fruit trees into all sorts of unusual forms, and this has been part of my gardening practice for three decades. However, although the craft skills and underlying principles of fruit pruning may be shared with that of ornamental trees, the guiding aesthetic is quite different. With fruit trees you are imposing a preconceived, artificial template on to the plant without any consideration of its genetically encoded natural form; it is all about domination and the expression of control. With creative pruning it is all about seeking to achieve whatever practical objectives you may have in such a way as to express and enhance the tree's inherent growth pattern. This is a more cooperative style of management that aims to identify the essence of the tree's character and enhance it whilst nudging it in the direction of your objectives, whether that be the separation of vegetation layers, admitting more light through or under the canopy, or showing off your subject's beautiful bark. To achieve this goal you need to spend time assessing the tree's overall character, especially its branch structure and pattern, any individual idiosyncrasies plus its relation to its surroundings. The highest accolade one can receive after carrying out such pruning is silence, because when it is skilfully implemented no one realizes you have done it: not a task for egotists! One of the most fascinating books on tree pruning that you can read is Jake Hobson's *Niwaki* (2007), all about training, pruning and shaping trees the Japanese way. Not really a template for the practice I am talking about, but an eye opener that illuminates western practice by shining a different light on it. As with children, the early years of a tree's life are most critical, and some timely and judicious formative pruning in its infancy will avoid the need to carry out more demanding and costly work later in life. Another advantage is that at this stage most work can be carried out on a decorator's stool or tripod ladder and using a pair of secateurs and a quality handsaw.

Top: While the branches of Carpinus betulus *'Fastigiata' are naturally ascendant we have nonetheless lifted its crown on a number of occasions to retain some definition between the tree and shrub layer and allow glimpses to the park.*

Bottom: The tracery of bare tree branches is one of the great joys of the winter garden. Each species, including the oaks, ash and swamp cypress present here, has its own pattern.

MAGNIFICENT MATURITY

In addition to the hundreds of young trees we have planted in the last twenty-seven years, West Dean has always been noted for its magnificent trees, and despite the depredations of storm and drought, we still have a good collection of mighty, mature specimens. These, of course, are long beyond formative pruning, and in general their management is more about supervising their decline in relation to public safety and extending their life for as long as possible. However, eventually they will begin to fail and we will have to remove them. We carry out much of this work ourselves, having both the expertise and machinery in-house to enable us to do so, but where necessary we will use selected contractors to undertake tree work that requires a climbing crew. While formative pruning is well within the remit of the average enthusiastic gardener with the right equipment, for more complicated work you are best advised to employ an Arboricultural Association kite-marked contractor.

'The planting of trees is not something to enter into lightly. The responsibilities are many, the pitfalls plentiful and the outcome uncertain, but a world without trees would be as unimaginable as a world without children. They are our future.'

*Unless it requires climbing we have always
undertaken our own tree work. Disposal is either
by logging up for firewood sales, burning on site
or chipping for mulching material.*

*When is a tree not a tree? Cherry laurel is normally
thought of as a hedging shrub. Allowed to mature it will reach
12 m/40 ft and nothing grows beneath it.*

Top, far left and left:
Metasequoia
glyptostroboides, *the dawn
redwood, is a charming
conical, deciduous conifer
with an attractive rufous
bark and a knotted trunk,
features that are highlighted
by judicious crown lifting.*

*Bottom: By progressive crown
lifting, we have allowed the
herbaceous underplanting to
thrive, shown off the trunk
and branch pattern and
framed a number of views. All
power to the pruning saw.*

PLEA FOR TREES

Despite having removed quite a large number of over-mature trees, our planting programme has far exceeded our removals. Given their scale and longevity, making the right choice of species is of particular importance. As with all planting, they need to be compatible with the ecology of your garden in terms of soil, drainage and moisture availability, but just as importantly they need to be able to do the job that you want them to do. Are they ultimately to be the next generation of magnificent trees framing long landscape views, offering expansive shade in high summer and a filigree of branches against a gelid sky, or an understorey tree whose canopy shuts down space, creates mid-height enclosure, and perhaps offers a blast of spring blossom to lift a late winter glade?

West Dean is a landscape that cries out for and can comfortably accommodate trees of the grandest stature, but I think that one of saddest trends to blight our under-resourced and impoverished public landscapes is the refusal to plant large urban trees for the future – a future where the ameliorating effects of large canopy trees will be ever more desirable. Instead, we are fed a diet of small, 'safe' and suburban blossom trees that may be momentarily uplifting for a brief season but will never achieve the dimensions capable of lifting the heart or cooling the environment for generations to come. It does not have to be this way. Go to the north-east seaboard of the USA and you will see towns that seem to be carved out of native woodland and where trees, buildings and humans happily coexist to the great benefit of the humans. The costs of proper tree management are just an accepted fact of life.

PLANTING TIPS FOR SUCCESSFUL ESTABLISHMENT

Sadly, where we do plant trees in our towns their survival rate is pretty low and their growth rate even lower. Which is frustrating because it is not rocket science, so here are my top tree planting tips.

~ Plant the right tree in the right place. Think about what its function is to be and what its cultural needs are (soil and pH) and select accordingly.
~ Buy the best stock available, and unless you have a very good reason for not doing so, plant as small as possible. If obtainable I will generally choose bare-root maidens (one-year-old single stems) or the smallest size up from that available. If the only stock available is potted, try to ensure they are not root-bound as their roots will tend to continue to spiral and not grow out, nor grown fast and too closely spaced as their stems will be as floppy as cheese sticks. It is well established that, ignoring any other specific factors, small bare-root saplings will establish more successfully than large pot-grown stock. It is also cheaper.
~ Contrary to what I was taught as a lad, do not dig a huge planting pit and fill it with the soil equivalent of crack cocaine. Trees are in it for

the long term and have to grow in the soil they are presented with, not be given a fast food takeaway meal for their formative years and then rapidly moved to a more austere diet as their roots leave the cloying comfort of their planting pit. Such pits also have a nasty habit of acting as drainage sumps and drowning their tender charges. All we do is prepare the area by spraying out a 1m/39inch-diameter round planting area and forking over the top spit and then plant the tree into the ground.

~ Do not fertilize the tree in its first year at least, as it will not have the root system to absorb the nutrients. Perhaps in subsequent years if your soil is particularly impoverished, but be guided by the amount of extension growth and feed only if it is not growing.

~ Keep a minimum area of 1 m/39 inches in all directions free of other vegetation. Do this for a minimum of five years. Grass is a very effective competitor for moisture and nutrients and will slow your tree's development considerably. This is the most important measure you can take to assist your establishing tree so do not ignore it. If you have some decent compost or woodchip, then mulch this area to a depth of 7.5 cm/3 inches, but keep the mulch a minimum of 5 cm/2 inches away from the base of the stem. This cordon sanitaire also has the effect of keeping brush cutters and mowers away from the young trunk; thousands of trees die every year because they are ringbarked by machinery.

~ If you plant small, robust trees they should be self-supporting and they should not need staking. If you do stake – and try not to – do so only to a height sufficient to stabilize the stem and root ball: generally no more than one-third the height of the tree.

~ Plant when the tree is dormant. If the following summer is hot and dry, it may be necessary to water, ideally every seven to ten days and in sufficient quantity to soak the whole root ball area to a good depth. After the first season it should not need watering as long as the 1 m/39 inch vegetation-free zone is maintained.

~ Carry out formative pruning from the start, but remember the leaves are the photosynthetic factories of growth so do not overdo it.

'Shrubs are not glamorous in the way that spring bulbs or iris are glamorous – but few gardens can exist without them.'
Monty Don

Shrubs

The border on the south-facing elevation of the house combines shrubs and herbaceous plants in a multi-layered picture. Rosa 'Fantin-Latour' in full bloom.

With the exception of the florally supercharged rhododendrons and roses, shrubs have always seemed dowdy and unglamorous, an air of drab spinsterdom lingering around their frowzy foliage. Whilst herbaceous plants have become chic, hip and happening, shrubs seem to be stuck in a subfusc Victorian villa garden where they hide the shed or obscure the neighbours, a life of worthy utility rather than designed delight. But this is pure prejudice that ignores the fact that shrubs are the Lego of the garden, the building blocks that enable you to paint backdrops, to create enclosure, to frame views and, yes, to screen the visually undesirable. Without their reassuring solidity and mass, a garden is a series of verticals (tree trunks) and floor covering (herbaceous plants and lawn) with nothing to knit it together or define its spaces on a human scale. On the downside they can also end up as amorphous clumps that meld into the canopy of trees, flop over associated herbaceous plantings, and generally dissipate definition and erase character by homogenizing the garden's disparate elements in their foliage embrace.

I have to confess that subliminally I share some of that bias, and if browsing a well-stocked gardening bookshelf rarely pick out a volume on shrubs as my first choice. However, experience has taught me their centrality in creating satisfying garden scenes, and over time I have

207

developed a palette of my favourites and also evolved strategies for their ongoing maintenance in such a way that they continue to perform for decades. This is an important point because I think that one of the reasons shrubs get a bad press is because generally we do not know how to manage them effectively.

Top: This was the old car park to the gardens twenty-five years ago! A typical West Dean planting with a herbaceous foreground, loose deciduous shrubs, topiarized evergreens and an open canopy of trees.

Bottom: Hydrangeas are an important part of our planting repertoire as they do well on our soil and give a good splash of colour later in the season. Hydrangea aspera Villosa Group provides a burst of rich purple alongside a real herbaceous stalwart, Polygonatum × hybridum.

THE SHRUB PROBLEM AND WHAT TO DO ABOUT IT

The problems begin at planting. If you employ a designer they will almost always grossly overplant, because most of their clients live life in the fast lane and do not want to wait to see the finished picture. So shrubs which might ultimately have a 4 m/13 ft spread get planted at 1 m/39 inches apart or less. Of course, this is predicated on the assumption that as the original planting matures it will be thinned to allow each plant to realize its full potential whilst rapidly achieving the desired closed canopy. Unfortunately, because of the focus on the instant results of the 'creative' design process over the perceived dullness of long-term maintenance, this rarely happens. The outcome is a shrubby Darwinian free-for-all where nobody gets to fully strut their stuff and display their potential. And let us be clear: this is not exclusive to designers. I (and I suspect most other gardeners) have been guilty of similar crimes against plants.

I suspect that this has something to do with the time frame in which shrubs live out their life cycles. Unlike herbaceous plants, they do not regenerate from scratch every year, making each spring a therapeutic opportunity to start over with a slate wiped clean. Equally, unlike trees they lack that 'reach for the sky' verticality that tends to rapidly remove their canopy from the horizontal human sight line. No, instead their almost invisible incremental growth does not really register for a few years and then boom: before you know it, your once tiny mites have turned into overbearing teenagers who have outgrown their allotted living quarters and are invading the family next door. So lesson number one is, if you have a maintenance schedule based on thinning to a final spacing over a number of years, then follow it! The work involved will ultimately be less than the neglectful alternative, and what is more you will fully realize the original desired design outcome.

The next issue with shrubs is that we tend to think of them as a low-maintenance solution requiring little or no ongoing input; whack them in, walk away and leave them to it. On one level and in certain situations that can work. I spent a couple of formative years divesting the shrubberies of Haringey Council of miscellaneous unsought adornments such as entire three-piece suites, and that was the only annual attention they received, yet they were still successfully fulfilling their function of screening playing fields or greening high-rise estates. In that situation they were green wallpaper designed to be seen from a distance and read en masse, functional if not inspirational. In a domestic garden and certainly at West Dean we have much higher expectations of what they will bring to the party. For them to achieve the desired results they need to be managed, and (assuming the normal inputs of adequate soil, nutrition and moisture levels plus absence of competition from weeds) that is primarily about

The distinctive character of bamboo helps to create the
slightly quirky atmosphere of the spring garden.

*Over time they can become very cluttered with
dead and dying stems. Thinning the clump by removing
these, plus a proportion of live culms, improves their
presence enormously.*

pruning, either to encourage flowering, a desired foliage or structural effect, or to keep them within their allotted bounds.

To deal with the last point first. As already alluded to, most of us – whether designer, professional manager or amateur gardener – overplant. Similarly we tend to plant for the short or medium term (two to ten years) but rarely for the long term (ten to a hundred years). As a consequence our shrub plantings, even if thinned appropriately, still ultimately tend to outgrow their locations. Either we do not trust them to grow as large as we know they might, or we rely on descriptions that give their size after only so many years, or we think that we will not be around to deal with them in their maturity. For whatever reason, the reality is that at some point most subjects will need to be constrained. In an ideal world this is achieved by early, regular and modest intervention whose impact is so low key it is almost invisible – definitely the preferred option. However, in the absence of such managerial perfection and confronted with a shrub that has long ago burst its breeches, one can always resort to the radical solution. One of the constant themes of this book is the forgiveness of nature and plants' all-conquering will to live. Most overgrown woody plants will respond well to being cut hard back or, perhaps even better, razed to the ground by rapidly regenerating a new structure within a couple of years. There are hazel coppices in East Anglia that are over a thousand years old and that have been coppiced every decade for all of that time, a comforting thought as you start up the chain saw to take an overgrown philadelphus or cotinus in hand. Such radical action is generally best carried out in late winter, when the plant is just coming out of dormancy, although on occasions I have performed the *coup de grâce* in midsummer with no ill effects.

'Whilst herbaceous plants have become chic, hip and happening, shrubs seem to be stuck in a subfusc Victorian villa garden where they hide the shed or obscure the neighbours, a life of worthy utility rather than designed delight. But this is pure prejudice.'

THE CUT SHRUB FORGIVES THE PRUNER

However, assuming you are well organized, temperamentally more attuned to minor manipulation over massive intervention, and the object of the exercise is to ensure a steady supply of flower at a suitable size, then the important thing to know is that most shrubs fall into one of three groups based on their flowering habits.

First, those which flower on the current season's growth, generally after midsummer. These are things like *Buddleja davidii* or *Hydrangea paniculata*, and are best pruned in early spring just as they come into growth, cutting back to the base of last year's wood. Hard pruning will produce vigorous growth with large flowers, light pruning twiggier growth with more but smaller flowers. Equally you can keep a low, almost sculptural framework by hard pruning or maintain a bigger, blowsier body by lighter pruning.

Second, those which flower on last season's wood, either early in the year and directly on last year's shoots, such as forsythia, or later in early summer on short laterals produced off last year's stems, like philadelphus. Either way, these are pruned immediately after flowering, removing the old stems either back to the main framework or to the ground.

Third, those which produce flowering spurs on older wood. This is

213

the basis of most fruit pruning (see the chapter on fruit) and is found in quite a range of shrubs, chaenomeles being a good example. The majority of this group need little pruning and can be kept in check and prolific by regularly pinching or stopping the growing tips through the season.

Generally we are reasonably good with dealing with Group One. They fit in well with the end of our winter work programme, we are well into the pruning groove having spent much of the winter trimming other things, whether trees, fruit, roses or topiary, and they are easy to identify and work on in their leafless dormant state. However, Group Two is more problematic. First, they have different flowering times and therefore cannot be dealt with in one hit. Second, they are much more awkward to work on in all their bosky fullness. And, third, there are a thousand other things crying out for attention at that time of the year. This means that all too often we miss the boat and end up resorting to the Sweeney Todd school of tonsorial trauma (see earlier paragraph on coppicing).

TOPIARY ON STEROIDS

All of the above principally relates to the management of deciduous shrub plantings. However, as important in creating the West Dean experience is the large legacy of Victorian evergreen shrub planting found throughout the grounds and arboretum. This is particularly significant in the winter months when its lustrous green foliage provides a welcome framework for the pared back landscape, but is equally important in summer as an anchoring solidity amongst the foam of foliage and flower. Without it an already rather nebulous *mise en scène* would be in danger of descending into an unstructured and unsatisfying froth; with it the place feels anchored and braced.

The primary constituents are Portugal and common laurel, yew, box and *Aucuba japonica*, historically all of them reliable if not over-exciting. This remains the case for the first three, but box is now under threat from box blight, and the vast majority of our substantial aucuba plantings (one has to wonder whether my late nineteenth-century predecessor bought a cheap, 'fell off the back of a hay-wain' job lot from a Victorian Arthur Daley) have all been dying over the last few years. We think this is probably the result of the terminal troika of old age, environmental stress (more extreme climatic conditions, especially increased drought and flooding) and thus increased susceptibility to honey fungus attack. Either way, it has created some excellent unplanned vistas that we have retained and offered the opportunity to pep up some previously gloomy corners with new shrubby planting, often the toughish but altogether jollier hydrangeas.

The problem with the trinity of (so far) sure-fire survivors, yew and the two laurels, is that left to their own devices and a little neglect they slowly turn from trimmed shrubs into trees, and by the time that anyone notices the undesired transformation, the prospect of tackling the metamorphosis has become too daunting and it is left to compound. This is exactly what had happened in some areas of the grounds, but especially in the broad acres of the arboretum where we were well on course to having the first laurel forest outside of the Caucasus.

To support the herbaceous clematis 'sentinels'
that punctuate the Yellow and Blue Border Anne builds some
mega hazel structures that eventually overshadow her!

The treatment has been to cut to the ground and remove by root grubbing in some areas (substantial areas in the arboretum), or to coppice and then progressively clip the regrowth until it has reached its final required proportions in others. The management yardstick is that all of this regenerated 'blobbery' should be trimmable from a decorator's stool – not much more than 2 m/7 ft in height – and be maintained with an annual haircut. What we now have is a rippling wave of evergreen that surges through the shrubberies as an internal linking theme and that, by partly emulating the rolling rises of our borrowed landscape of the surrounding South Downs, connects us to the wider terrain.

This theme of super-sized topiary is also manifested in our tendency to perform a rather more high-rise version on some very large shrubs, hedges and trees. Because this requires getting the cherry picker out and is quite time consuming, we try to reserve it for special subjects that have a high impact and we only do it on a two-year cycle, stretched to three years if we think we can get away with it. In contrast, the smaller pieces, principally box or yew – high profile, viewed from close up and more intricately shaped – benefit from a theoretical twice yearly cut but because of circumstances do not always get it!

'Without the reassuring solidity and mass of shrubs, a garden is a series of verticals (tree trunks) and floor covering (herbaceous plants and lawn) with nothing to knit it together or define its spaces on a human scale.'

VERTICAL GARDENING

West Dean also has an awful lot of wall or frame trained plants. These range from the *Magnolia grandiflora* and ornamental vines on the front of the house, through the numerous roses and clematis on the pergola, to the pyracanthas and the *Cotoneaster horizontalis* that dress various walls in the garden. Some plants are self-clinging such as ivy and Virginia creeper, but generally the foundation of all effective vertical gardening is to ensure that you have a strong, serviceable support system in place. This generally consists of tensioned wires at 30 cm/12 inch spacings and held in place (3 cm/1¼ inches off the wall to allow for air circulation and tying in) by vine eyes driven into the mortar. This is quite a job in itself, particularly on a building the size of West Dean House, but without it your climbers will soon descend to become ground creepers, a very different outcome from that desired.

The most splendid example of vertical gardening at West Dean is the 100m/328ft-long Peto pergola that bestrides the north lawn. This has sixty columns along its length and is 'roofed' with a framework that resembles a high-level wooden railway. Each column has at least one climbing subject on it, many two, and these are all carefully trained around the columns and then over and along the wooden framework. The net effect of all this effort is to create a dreamy, scent-laden elongated bower along which the visitor wafts in a sensory soaked reverie whilst gazing out through the framework of columns on to a series of shifting, flower framed views. We hope it provides a rich return on the considerable investment of time and effort involved in its annual maintenance: six weeks of demounting, pruning and retying that is the annual winter overhaul, which is then followed by the constant tying in of extension growth through the spring and summer. Not all buildings are improved by a touch of vertical gardening, but from our point of view they are few and far between.

Perennials and bulbs

If trees are the monoliths of the garden providing verticality and aerial enclosure and shrubs the building blocks of spatial definition, then herbaceous perennials and bulbs are the unifying carpet that links those spaces at ground level. But first define your terms: just what is a herbaceous perennial or bulb?

Well, unsurprisingly, a perennial is a plant that continues its growth from year to year. Woody perennials – the aforementioned shrubs and trees – have a permanent above-ground woody structure that forms the starting point for each year's new growth. In contrast, the aerial parts of most herbaceous perennials die down each autumn, to be replaced the next spring by new shoots that emerge phoenix-like from the perennating rootstock. Bulbs and corms, which are both variations on a modified stem, can be classified as herbaceous perennials in that they also exhibit that cycle of growth, senescence, dormancy and regrowth from a subterranean organ. This life cycle is an adaptation to the vagaries of climate with the plant becoming dormant when conditions are inimical to growth. In northern latitudes this will generally be in winter when the plants effectively hibernate like bears, but in warmer regions it is more often a response to the heat or drought of summer when they aestivate, like some

In May, the emerging herbaceous planting of the dry garden is animated by the vivid chromatic drumsticks of Allium 'Purple Sensation'.

fish and amphibians. The majority of bulbs belong to this group with many hailing from the Near and Middle East.

This definition highlights one of the most attractive characteristics of herbaceous plants, which is that each year they give both us, as well as themselves, a winter rest: effectively a form of visual detox. However, by late winter we once more crave the reappearance of their fresh and pristine foliage, whose rapid cycle of growth and development is a source of daily excitement and joy through to early summer. Then comes the pleasure of their varied and colourful flower displays, and even in their slow slide to quiescence they can be strangely attractive. For me herbaceous plants are as much about their foliage as their flowers. With a few exceptions most species' floral display lasts from three to six weeks at the outside, whereas the foliage can provide a subtle but still captivating show for the whole season. Let the foliage force be with you!

HERBACEOUS HISTORIES

The fortunes of herbaceous perennials have varied over the last two centuries. Before the 1860s they were deeply unfashionable and consigned either to the utilitarian cutting border or to the social outer darkness of the labourer's cottage garden. The change in their status began with William Robinson's championing of perennials as a vital component of a naturalistic garden in his ground-breaking *The Wild Garden* of 1870. This was consolidated and domesticated in *The English Flower Garden* (1883) and then reinforced by Gertrude Jekyll's advocacy of their more formal use in her tightly structured, carefully colour-coordinated and rigorously managed herbaceous borders as described in *Colour Schemes for the Flower Garden* (1908). From the zenith of those Edwardian gardens of a golden afternoon, they have metamorphosed through various permutations, principally the hybrid mixed border and variants such as Adrian Bloom's advocacy of island beds. However, even in my gardening youth the Jekyllian border still retained its nostalgic grip on the English psyche, enjoying a series of mini-revivals in the 1970s and 1980s under the tutelage of luminaries such as Graham Stuart Thomas and Rosemary Verey.

The border bastion only began to crumble under successive waves of influence from Europe and North America, where advocates such as the German nurseryman Karl Foerster and American designers Wolfgang Oehme and James van Sweden reimagined the border by advocating a wider palette of herbaceous plants (including ferns and grasses) and used them in a more naturalistic way by planting broad swathes over large areas. That initial rising tide has now become a positive storm surge with the current crop of international designers, such as Piet Oudolf, Nigel Dunnett, James Hitchmough, Keith Wiley and Noel Kingsbury, all seeking inspiration from the aesthetics and ecological dynamics of natural plant communities and adapting these to create sustainable designed landscapes in both private gardens and public spaces.

Top: Matching size and type of planting to the scale, proportions and character of the space that it occupies is a vital part of an effective design. As a consequence nothing in the intimate space of the sunken garden gets any higher than 60 cm/2 ft with much of it being prostrate or cushion forming.

Bottom: The restricted colour palette and repetition of plants help to give the area a strong and distinctive character.

The 'Crazies Corner' planting in the spring garden consists
of plants with distinctive architectural form. A percentage of these are
not hardy and have to be lifted in the autumn and overwintered
under cover, but given its impact and the small scale of the planting,
we think it is a justifiable luxury.

*Most of our bulb planting is permanent and naturalized
in grass. But the changing annual display of container-grown
bulbs lights up the walled garden with colour and interest when
little else is flowering.*

'If trees are the monoliths of the garden providing verticality and aerial enclosure and shrubs the building blocks of spatial definition, then herbaceous perennials and bulbs are the unifying carpet that links those spaces at ground level.'

BORDERS WITH A BLAST

Herbaceous plants have always been favourites of mine and are a mainstay of our borders at West Dean. Characteristically our approach to their use is an amalgam of all the styles just mentioned. Over the last two decades the garden has evolved to resemble a tranquil piece of music with lots of pianissimo sub-themes. The bulk of the herbaceous planting is relatively subdued, forming a close-knit matrix and mainly reliant on foliage for long-term effect. However, on occasion that leafy underlying drone crescendos to a lively climax through the floral fireworks of the pergola, sunken garden, and herbaceous and mixed borders in various locations.

Given the garden's roots in the Victorian pomp and circumstance of high input/high outcome horticulture, it is unsurprising that we still have a pretty large commitment to the sub-Jekyllian pure(ish) herbaceous flower border. These are principally found within the walled garden and are contemporary adaptations of the cutting borders that historically occupied their locations. They are all double borders flanking either side of one of the axial paths and are all backed by a black-painted mild steel framework. This supports a range of clematis and roses in the two fruit garden borders and apple and pear espaliers in the kitchen garden, a backdrop that acts as botanical understudy to the main floral performance.

As we have such an extended period of interest within the walled garden, we felt justified in creating three colour-themed borders within that space which are chromatically intense but whose impact is relatively short-lived: midsummer to mid-autumn. Given the kitchen garden's complete visual isolation, its sunny south-facing aspect and the calm green background of the vegetables, we felt that this location could absorb a real visual blast. Hence the Hot Border, 34 m/112 ft × 2 m/7 ft, a riot of red, yellow, orange, crimson, gold and all points between that divides the site in half on a north–south axis. This is at its most photogenic during the most popular visiting months of July and August, when these vibrant, joyful colours elicit a fantastically positive response and instantly set camera shutters whirring.

In the fruit garden we have the Rose Border, 50 m/164 ft × 3 m/10 ft, running north–south, which combines old-fashioned shrub roses and herbaceous planting with a pastel palette of pinks, mauves and soft blues and is at its peak in June–July. Bisecting it, running east–west and with the thatched round apple store as eye-stopper at its eastern end, the self-explanatory Yellow and Blue Border, 54 m/177 ft × 2.25 m/7½ ft, takes over from July to September, by which time the ripening fruit continues the autumn display.

PREPARATION AND PERSONNEL

So what are the principal factors that make for successful herbaceous plantings? As always, that can have various answers depending on your objectives, but in our high-profile areas it is lavish inputs. Because herbaceous plants grow so intensely and are relatively long lived, they are

hungry feeders, and the soil must provide the fuel on which the high-octane performance depends. As with all our new beds we generally keep an area fallow for up to a year before planting, depending on circumstances. This gives us the opportunity to incorporate a generous amount of compost, generally a minimum of a 15 cm/6 inch layer, into the bed and also to ensure that it is weed free, particularly of noxious thugs like ground elder or bindweed. To plant a border into an area infested with any such botanical bully boy is to condemn oneself to a lifetime of Sisyphean heartache as your treasures sink beneath a tide of invasive alien foliage. To avoid this misery we roughly cultivate the area on five or six occasions through the growing season, water it in periods of drought, and regularly spray off with glysophate any growth that occurs.

Having laid your foundation, the next stage is to assemble your team. The subject of plant selection is worthy of a book on its own, so suffice it to say that it must be fit for purpose. As already indicated, we have two main types of herbaceous planting. One acts as green wallpaper, principally chosen for foliage and architectural effect and in combination with shrubs and trees; the other for floral fizz, mainly chosen for flower colour combinations and where foliage is of little significance. What they both have in common is the need for their component parts to mesh together both visually (whether colour or form) and physically, to create a self-sustaining, dense and continuous matrix that requires minimum intervention. To achieve that result requires both an artistic eye with a talent for aesthetically pleasing juxtaposition and a practical understanding of the growth structure and vigour of each plant so as to produce a closed, balanced canopy without any of its constituents being suppressed by any other.

Top: A relatively small proportion, no more than a third, of our herbaceous plantings require staking. The secret lies in a good supply of hazel, an early intervention and a talent for weaving!

Bottom: Herbaceous plants put on astonishing amounts of rapid growth once they get going and any staking is quickly swallowed up by the foliage flood. Geranium psilostemon *rapidly subsuming its hazel corset.*

STUDY AND SUPPORT

With the best will in the world, no planting plan ever works perfectly; some plants prove feeble, others rampant, some flop, some run, all of which means that an annual performance review is vital. This is ongoing throughout the growing season, but is collated and recorded when the display is at its peak to be acted on at the appropriate time, depending on the action advised. It is this continuous attention to detailed and subtle editing that will ensure the longevity of a planting. Of our five floral semi-herbaceous borders, two have been completely lifted and renovated but only after a couple of decades, whilst the others have undergone minor, incremental change, a credit to their initial layout and ongoing maintenance.

After two or three years, when the reserve of nutrients in the original soil begins to decline, the pre-growing season starts with the application of a fertilizer base dressing of Fish, Blood and Bone followed by a light mulch of 4 cm/1½ inches of well-rotted compost. The young growth easily penetrates this, and as it starts to unfurl and expand the annual round of staking commences. This is a time-consuming and skilled task and is therefore only applied to those plants that absolutely need it, probably no more than a third of the inhabitants. With our small area of hazel coppice we are self-sufficient in staking material. Anne Kelly, who has an

*Some elements of the borders are not fully hardy and have
to be lifted each autumn. Cannas are one of these.*

Surplus leaves are removed and the clump is split into
manageable bits which are potted up and then stored in a
frost-free glasshouse to slowly senesce.

arts background and is the gardener principally in charge of the borders, has developed a staking system that combines military efficiency with sculptural nous and that has made our staking as much a part of the visitors' enjoyment as the plants it supports. The secrets of her success lie in her innate talent, a generous supply of good staking material, an intimate understanding of each subject's requirements and correct timing. An early start, March–April, is critical and as plants reach around 20 cm/8 inches high, so their annual support system is installed. Leave it too late and it is like trying to herd cats.

'With the best will in the world no planting plan ever works perfectly; some plants prove feeble, others rampant, some flop, some run, all of which means that an annual performance review is necessary.'

THE KINDEST CUT

Next off the rank comes the 'Chelsea chop'. This is the technique of cutting back the plant's early growth by a third to a half in mid-May. The object is to reduce the mature dimensions of the plant and to delay flowering. The outcome is to reduce staking, prevent flopping, and delay and increase the number (whilst generally reducing the individual size) of flowers. *Helenium* 'Lemon Queen', an important contributor to the Yellow and Blue Border for its late starburst of citrine-coloured flowers, was simply too tall, over 2.5 m/8 ft, for the scale of the border until we discovered that by staking it to 1.25 m/4 ft and then cutting it back to the top of the stakes in late May it would flower at a much more modest 1.8 m/6 ft: bingo!

Because of the many variables involved in plants' response to this practice, it is impossible to make hard and fast rules, but suffice it to say it has a long and successful pedigree and every garden has to develop its own corpus of practice based on its unique set of circumstances.

Related to this is the practice of cutting plants back to the ground after flowering with the aim of producing, at a minimum, a fresh flush of foliage but with the potential bonus of another burst of bloom. We make extensive use of this technique in the 'green carpet' planting throughout the grounds, which is biased towards spring and early summer growth and flowering. Untouched, these would be looking very dishevelled by midsummer but are easily resurrected by razing to the ground: the kindest cut of all! Subjects such as geraniums and that ubiquitous West Dean 'doer' *Trachystemon orientalis* respond really well, whereas another tough favourite, *Polygonatum × hybridum*, makes no comeback whatsoever. As with the Chelsea chop it is an educated and pragmatic 'suck it and see'.

Another form of cutting that goes on from first flowering until mid-autumn is dead-heading, the removal of spent flower heads. This has a number of benefits ranging from improving the plant's appearance (some flowers, such as dahlias for instance, look terrible as they decay), through significantly extending the flowering and growth period by redirecting its energy from reproduction to further flower production, to preventing unwanted self-seeding. Generally we have a relatively low tolerance to self-seeding, as weeding seedlings out of a dense border is a time-consuming and demoralizing task that we can ill afford. Dead-heading is probably the most time-consuming job in the calendar and one which you must stay on top of if it is not going to become an insuperable

I love the 'end of pier' bounciness of dahlias but they
can't be accused of dying gracefully. Regular dead-heading
through the season is a must.

*Herbaceous plants definitely benefit from a winter haircut
to remove last season's dying foliage and allow the emerging
foliage to be seen in all its pristine promise.*

obstacle. We only achieve this through the dexterous input of nimble volunteers. The only seed heads spared the chop are those which are an attractive feature in themselves, such as *Phlomis russelliana* or nigella.

IN THE BLEAK MIDWINTER

In recent years it has become popular to sing the praises of the beauty of decaying herbaceous plants and to a degree I can see the point, although I think our wet, mild maritime climate tends to rapidly reduce old herbaceous vegetation to a compost heap on legs rather than the austere, skeletal, frost-rimed beauty of North American or continental gardens. As a consequence we tend to clear the borders in one fell swoop and at a time that suits our work schedule rather than any other arbitrary point. Another example of professional hard-nosedness over dubious aesthetics.

Finally, in the dead of winter when all is sere and supine, plants can be lifted, split and repositioned as per your earlier midsummer observations for improvement and editing. Equally, those plants that are losing their youthful vigour can be regenerated by the same process of lifting, splitting and then discarding the senile clump centres and replanting the vigorous outer edges.

BULBOUS BOUNTY

Alongside herbaceous plants, bulbs are another of my favourites. Nothing lifts the heart in the seemingly endless depths of winter as the sighting of the first snowdrop flowers, followed in rapid succession by aconites, crocus, tulips and the whole bulbous panoply. Their early flowering is one of their big attractions, enlivening the garden when little else is in bloom. Equally appealing is their relative cheapness. Pound for pound I think they are tremendous value, and particularly so if you view your plantings as an initial investment that will pay generous and continuous compound interest as they bulk up and spread by offsets and seeding. This, of course, requires a degree of patience, but part of the pleasure of proper gardening is delighting in the deferred satisfaction gained from attuning yourself to the rhythms of mother nature.

It is fair to say that, unlike herbaceous plants, bulbs are floral peacocks – all about flower power – whose foliage is neutral at best or an eyesore at worst, particularly as it messily dies off just as the garden bursts into new life. However, because we tend to naturalize them in our wildflower meadows, this is not too much of an issue; their fading leaves are disguised by the rapidly developing foliage of the surrounding grasses and herbaceous plants. Grown in this way they are also astonishingly trouble free. Once planted you can forget about them except to ensure that they are allowed to build up next season's reserves and flower buds by allowing them to photosynthesize for as long as possible. Do not 'tidy' their leaves until they start to shrivel; they are the food factory for the plant. As I have already described the West Dean way of bulb planting in the chapter on lawns, I will say no more on that.

Top left to bottom, clockwise: From the early promise of an emerging ornamental rhubarb leaf, through the freshness and innocence of a dense mat of lily of the valley to the strong, all-season presence of clumps of agapanthus foliage followed by the late summer floral fizz of their spikes of rich blue flowers, herbaceous plants are a stalwart of West Dean's garden scene.

Left: Narcissus *'February Gold'* (which in my experience always flowers in March) *and* Chionodoxa *'Pink Giant' combined with burgundy* Helleborus orientalis *provide a cheerful welcome to the sunken garden.*

Below: Narcissus *'Jenny' brightening the scene on the Picnic Lawn. Earlier this would have been a sea of snowdrops, followed by* Crocus tommasinianus, Scilla siberica *leading into* Fritillaria meleagris *and finally* Camassia esculenta *in May. Plus, of course, a succession of wild flowers until cutting in early July.*

With the exception of the pergola, sunken garden and dry garden we have steered clear of bulb planting in beds in any quantity, but this may be an area for future development. However, each year we do mount quite extensive displays of potted bulbs in the walled garden and glasshouses. These are potted up in early autumn, heavily watered and then moved to an open-fronted shed on a north-facing wall where they will overwinter. This cool, shaded spot is the consistently coldest location we can provide for them, and this environment is perfect for allowing them to come into slow growth. When their 'noses' emerge they are moved to another north-facing location but in the open, and when ready to flower from there to their display position. It is a straightforward enough operation, and the main trick is to ensure that you have an appropriate number of suitable species and varieties to cover the display season from January with the first snowdrops to the last of the tulips in May. *Floreat bulbocodium*!

'What wondrous life is this I lead!
Ripe apples drop about my head;
The luscious clusters of the vine
Upon my mouth do crush their wine;
The nectarine and curious peach,
Into my hands themselves do reach;
Stumbling on melons, as I pass,
Ensnared with flowers, I fall on grass.'
Andrew Marvell , 'The Garden'

The Fruit Garden

'Cherry Walk' is a south-facing wall in the pit yard that has seven fan-trained cherries along its length. The trees are beautiful in blossom but it's blackbirds that benefit most from the fruit.

Ever since Adam ate the apple, the image of the orchard as a symbol of a post-lapsarian return to innocent harmony seems to have been hot-wired into our psyches, a metaphysical mantra that emerges as a source of succour at times of stress. Andrew Marvell's poetic meditation on the superiority of a contemplative life lived close to Edenic nature, as opposed to the follies of worldly ambition played out amidst the falsities of court and city, is just one of many evocations of the fruit garden as a supreme expression of a life well-lived.

Perhaps one of the reasons for their potency as an image of contentment and well-being was that, by their very nature, orchards could only thrive in an ordered and stable society where people were able to invest the decades of time and effort required to bring them to abundant maturity. Thus, the story of fruit growing in the British Isles really begins with the settled civic conditions of the Roman occupation, when many of our favourite fruits such as the apple, plum and cherry were first imported and systematically cultivated. With the departure of the legions in AD 410 and the ensuing chaos of the successive waves of Germanic and Scandinavian invaders, the art of fruit growing was lost, only to be revived with the establishment of the great monasteries, whose educated,

245

inquisitive inhabitants and structured, stable life lent itself to the art of gardening and fruit growing.

Oblique cordons are a fantastic way of growing a large number of varieties in a small space. Eighteen pear varieties are grown on a 20 m/65 ft length of wall.

....

A FRUITFUL TRADITION

From then to the present the story of fruit cultivation has been one of steady progress, with continuous improvement in fruit varieties, growing techniques, storage and distribution. Ultimately this has led to the astonishing cornucopia that is the contemporary supermarket fruit counter, where a bewildering range of perfectly presented fruit, virtually without regard to season, is offered to the too often jaded consumer. However, as in so many aspects of horticulture, it was the nineteenth century that ushered in fruit growing's golden age, both in the domestic garden and in the commercial plantation. The founding of the Horticultural Society of London in 1804 and the Royal Caledonian Horticultural Society soon afterwards initiated a renaissance in all aspects of gardening, with their meetings, gardens, publications and shows rapidly becoming a vital source of information on the latest aspects of fruit growing and with membership being de rigueur for any self-respecting professional gardener or interested landowner. Rich landowners would vie with each other in trying to produce the earliest pineapples or the most luscious muscat grapes whilst the great nurserymen of the day, such as Thomas Rivers and Thomas Laxton, greatly extended the range and availability of new and improved varieties of both tender and hardy fruit. Nevertheless, the huge improvements in the standard of Victorian garden fruit growing can principally be attributed to the great estate gardeners of that period, such as Joseph Paxton of Chatsworth or James Barnes at Bicton. Having learnt their trade via a long apprenticeship, their knowledge was extended and deepened as they moved from garden to garden as journeymen. By the time they became foreman of the fruit garden or even head gardener, they had mastered the intricacies of their trade and were as happy growing figs under glass as training, tying in or thinning all those miles of walls of fan-trained trees that formed one of the chief glories of the Victorian walled garden in its heyday.

....

THE FRUIT GARDEN DISPLAYED

The walled garden at West Dean was part of that tradition, as evidenced by the vast range of glass given over to the production of out-of-season and exotic fruit and the extensive wall-trained fruit mentioned above. In addition, there were two further orchards of top fruit, outside of but adjacent to the walled garden, where extensive supplies of apples and pears were also grown. However, with the notable exception of two veteran figs and two gnarled glasshouse grapes, all evidence of that legacy had disappeared by the early 1990s.

At the heart of our plan for rejuvenating the garden was the reanimation of the walled garden as a productive space firmly in the mould of its nineteenth-century antecedents but adapted to the

Whether highly trained goblets and pyramids or
half-standards, all well-grown fruit relies on decisive formative
pruning and thenceforth a regular and appropriate annual
pruning regime.

It takes a minimum of seven years to produce a
four-winged pyramid or goblet but the wait is worth it
in every season once established.

circumstances and resources of the late twentiety century. Naturally a fruit collection formed a significant part of that plan. The principal aims of the collection were to grow:

~ as extensive a range of top and soft fruit, both outdoors and under glass, as was compatible with the resources available to manage them to as high a standard as possible;

~ any variety (assuming availability) that was recorded as having been grown at West Dean between 1890 and 1914, the zenith of the walled garden's activity and the approximate period of the tenure of Mr and Mrs William James (Edward James's parents);

~ a broad selection of Victorian varieties, as this was both the period of the walled garden's development and also a golden age for the development of new varieties;

~ both earlier and twentieth-century cultivars so as to display and compare as extensive a range as possible;

~ all of these in as many diverse ways as possible, including half-standards, four-winged pyramids, goblets, oblique cordons, espaliers, palmette verriers and any other feasible variations.

We now have a collection of 100 varieties of apples, 45 of pears and good collections of peaches, nectarines, cherries and plums. All of the fruit was planted in 1993–4 and is now fully mature. As with all of our garden developments, our priority was to create a place of beauty for the eye and solace for the soul, then to inspire and gently educate our visitors, and finally to produce a useful crop of fruit.

'Historically each outdoor wall was reserved for the fruits best adapted to its particular microclimate. On the south-facing wall were peaches, nectarines and apricots – all lovers of sunlight and heat.'

LOCATION, LOCATION, LOCATION

In the main we have followed our forebears' example in terms of location and selection of different fruit types. Historically each outdoor wall was reserved for the fruits best adapted to its particular microclimate. On the south-facing wall were peaches, nectarines and apricots – all lovers of sunlight and heat. However, after a decade of growing very fine peaches and nectarines under glass and very poor ones outside, mainly because of the scourge of leaf curl in the peaches and dieback in the apricots, we decided to accept the inevitable and converted that space to a much more rewarding fig wall. The west-facing wall tended to grow plums and pears, the east wall plums and Morello cherries, and cooking plums on the cool and shady north wall. This particular wall's construction is of interest as it is a 'crinkle-crankle' wall and, unusually, is angular and zigzag as opposed to the more usual wavy serpentine. The rationale behind its design was to economize on bricks and therefore construction costs; you can build a thinner wall to a greater height because of the stabilizing effect of its configuration. In addition, you achieve more wall length in a given run, plus the reflective niches on its south side were also seen to provide an especially favourable environment for heat lovers. Most of the wall-trained fruit are grown as fans, although some are double or 'U' cordons.

A GARDEN FOR FRUIT

The greatest departure from precedent within the walls was the conversion of the 0.4 hectare/1 acre lower walled garden from what was historically kitchen garden to an orchard of traditional half-standard apple trees underplanted with a wildflower meadow. These have been grown as traditional open-crown trees and are kept to a height of approximately 3.5 m/12 ft to facilitate picking. Roughly a quarter of them are local Sussex varieties such as 'Doctor Hogg' and 'Crawley Reinette'. The other innovation in this area is the collection of ornately trained pears and cooking apples growing in the grassed border at the base of the walls. These are either goblets or four-winged pyramids, both forms based on the pruning principles of Louis Lorette, a French fruit grower of the late nineteenth century. These tightly and ornately trained forms rely on the propensity of apples, pears, plums and cherries to fruit on short spurs induced by summer pruning. However, a small number of varieties are tip bearers: they fruit on the current season's extension growth. Summer prune these and you will be condemned to a cycle of sterility as you will assiduously remove the fruiting wood when you summer prune. Obviously, these do not lend themselves to trained forms!

PRUNING FOR PSEUDS

Fruit pruning tends to be unnecessarily shrouded in mystery. Like any craft it takes time and practice to master, but it is not as arcane as most people think. There are a few things to remember when approaching the subject for the first time. First, plants are desperate to survive, thrive and propagate the species, and will almost certainly cling to life despite all our abuse. Second, most trees germinate, develop, propagate and die without any human intervention; we prune to achieve certain human objectives, not because the tree needs us to do so for them to flourish. Third, there are just a few basic principles; grasp these and you are well on the way. *Fruit* (1988, still available second-hand on the Internet), written by Harry Baker, Fruit Superintendent at RHS Wisley for many years, has been my well-thumbed fruit-growing bible for decades. Invest in a copy and follow its concise and clearly illustrated instructions and you will not go far wrong. Fourth, most people are far too tentative: spare the blade and spoil the tree. Fifth, as with children, the formative years (anything from three to seven years depending on the form) are the critical ones. Invest the time then and it will pay dividends for decades later.

THE ANNUAL ROUND

So how does a year in the fruit garden evolve? The first job of the new season is to prune all of the half-standard apple trees, nearly 100, before Christmas. The urgency has nothing to do with the trees' needs but rather with that of the wildflower sward beneath them. This is packed with

*Soft fruit is another element of fruit production
at West Dean. Here's Shaun wrestling with pruning
and tying in blackberries after fruiting.*

As with so many things, having a robust support system
is vital. Soft fruit is semi-permanent, a minimum of a decade
in one position, so it's a reasonable investment over that
time frame.

....

'By early April the greenhouse grapes, grown on a rod-and-spur system, have put on sufficient growth to allow the shoots to be thinned, one shoot to a wire, and trained laterally along it.'

snowdrops and crocuses that, in the warm microclimate of the walled garden, can be in flower by mid-January, and they would be damaged by a gardener's feet stomping all over them. The object of the pruning is to keep the trees at a suitable height, 3.5 m/12 ft, for ease of picking, to allow light and air into the crowns, and to keep them fruitful by renewal pruning, which replaces a large proportion of the non-framework wood on a three-year cycle.

Once this is complete, all of the trained fruit are given a once-over and any outstanding pruning and tying in are dealt with. By mid-February the peaches and nectarines under glass are coming into flower, at which point their pruning and tying in are checked for any anomalies and the ritual of their artificial pollination begins. Because there is little insect activity at this time of the year, it is traditional to mimic the beneficial busyness of the bee by transferring pollen from one flower to another using a rabbit's tail attached to a cane: very therapeutic and pays dividends in lots of lovely juicy fruit. On a commercial orchard the spraying season would be under way, but although we are not organic, we do little or no spraying most seasons. This is mainly because it is time consuming and expensive and we can produce a decent and presentable crop without it.

By early April the greenhouse grapes, grown on a rod and spur system, have put on sufficient new growth to allow the shoots to be thinned, one shoot to a wire, and trained laterally along it. This process continues until there is a closed canopy covering the interior of the glasshouse roof. Until they have set their fruit, vines are extremely vigorous and left to their own devices would soon become a nightmare of rampant, unproductive growth. This is only prevented by constant pinching out of all sub-lateral shoots to one leaf until the end of the growing season. By late April the flower trusses are developed, and these are then thinned to leave one bunch on every third lateral. Allowing too much fruit formation can weaken the vine and is not sustainable. From June onwards the grapes swell quickly and must be heavily thinned – taking out up to 70 per cent – to allow them space to develop fully. This is one of the most time-consuming, neck-cricking and least favourite tasks in the calendar, but without it the bunches would be congested and poor at best or collapse in a fermenting heap of fungal spores at worst. The sweetener, literally, is anticipating picking them when fully mature in October, by which time they have become taste grenades of honeyed richness.

One of the most magical periods in the orchard year is May: blossom time. Everything is fresh and verdant, and the riot of fruit blossom is complemented by the sheets of cowslips beneath the trees – a scene of blissful fecundity that, in the absence of any destructive late frosts, will soon result in an abundance of embryonic fruit. Nature is wildly profligate, solely focused on the reproduction of its genes and not in the least bit interested in producing Grade A fruit. If all of the potential fruit were allowed to mature, you would end up with a glut of small, not very attractive examples that would exhaust the tree and probably induce biennial bearing. The tree has a built-in thinning mechanism, the so-called 'June drop', but this needs to be supplemented by vigorous hand thinning when the fruit is the size of a walnut, leaving each one 15–23 cm/6–9 inches apart. In my experience very few people are remotely ruthless enough at this; however, something is definitely better than nothing.

259

*Harvesting fruit is a skill in itself with timing in
relation to each variety's maturation being a significant factor.
David, a volunteer, became quite an expert over time.*

*For over two decades we staged a weekend Apple Show
every October. One of the highlights was always a display
of the 100 or so varieties we grow.*

With peaches and nectarines under glass fruit drop happens far earlier, probably early April. At a similar time their new shoots need to be thinned and loosely tied in. Because they do not produce spurs like apples and pears, instead fruiting on last season's wood, they are pruned on a replacement system: a new shoot is selected to replace the branch that is currently bearing young fruit. When these have matured and been picked, the old branch that was bearing them is pruned out and the selected current season's shoot tied in place to replace it. As always, it is simple in theory but slightly more challenging in practice.

With the trained apples and pears, other than fruit thinning the big mid-season job is summer pruning. There are lots of variations on the exact methodology and timing, but under our conditions and with our primarily aesthetic objectives our method, broadly speaking, consists of cutting back all new laterals and sub-laterals to one bud above the basal cluster around mid-June. By this time the new growth can be up to 50 cm/20 inches long, and any sense that the tree is a carefully trained form is smothered in a tsunami of juvenile shoots. A hard haircut reimposes a sense of order and decorum as well as encouraging the tree to redirect its energy into producing next year's fruit buds as opposed to riotous vegetative growth. However, by mid-September the lords of vegetative misrule have once more taken over and the whole process is repeated again.

And then all that remains is to harvest the overflowing fruits of your labour. This can begin with soft fruit, peaches, nectarines and figs in June and July segueing into plums and cherries in late July and August, and then apples and pears from mid-August to the first frosts. A crowning glory before the cycle starts once more.

'Teach a man to fish and he eats for a day.
Teach a man to garden and the whole
neighbourhood gets tomatoes!'
Anon.

The Productive Garden

For me the kitchen garden is defined by its serried ranks of well-grown vegetables, as handsome as any herbaceous border and twice as tasty.

All of us are the product of our upbringing, an influence that moulds us for the rest of our lives. Although a Londoner born and bred, as a child I was fortunate enough to spend at least one weekend a month staying in my grandparents' 400-year-old cottage in rural Essex. Here I would 'help' them to tend their respective horticultural domains. The garden was long and relatively narrow, protected by a neatly clipped 1.5m/5ft-high hawthorn hedge and divided into two uneven parts. The smaller area (roughly one-third) was Nan's world, a billowy, flowery cottage garden populated by all of the old-fashioned favourites garnered as 'slips' and divisions from friends' gardens. All very flowery, all very nice, but not half as captivating as the serried ranks of vegetables lined up with parade ground precision on the other side of the path. This was the disciplined and productive kingdom of Grandad, whose gardening style reflected his military service in the First World War and the exactitude of his trade, bricklaying. It was the productive garden in earnest, a serious enterprise that put food on the table and pickles in the preserving pan. This unselfconscious self-sufficiency was borne out of pride and need in equal measure, and embedded itself in my psychological DNA as the essence of the 'Good Life' long before its television namesake reinvented it as a lifestyle choice for the *bien pensants*. If that land of lost content was borne out of William Cobbett's early nineteenth-century *Cottage Economy* and the tradition of working-class independence, West Dean's 1 hectare/ 2.5 acre walled kitchen garden is very much in the lineage of Loudon and McIntosh and the great country house garden: definitely more 'To the Manor Born' than 'The Good Life'. However, what links these social opposites is the desire to supply their respective households with as comprehensive a range of quality crops for as long a season as possible and as their resources allow.

....

A VEGETABLE EDEN

At West Dean those resources were, and are, quite considerable. Like most walled gardens it is on a south-facing, gentle slope that is both a suntrap and a frost drain. Its 3m/10ft-high flint and brick walls keep miscreants out, mitigate the influence of the wind, and act as a heat sink whose radiant reservoir is released overnight and can keep temperatures a degree or two higher than those outside their balmy embrace. Add to that a soil which has been almost continuously cultivated and cared for over two centuries and you have the ingredients for some supercharged vegetable growing.

The contemporary 0.25 hectare/two-thirds of an acre kitchen garden is watched over by the substantial nineteenth-century Bothy, purpose built by a benevolent Willie James, where generations of garden apprentices 'lived in', surrounded by the backdrop of their labours. The area is laid out on the classic Victorian pattern of two central intersecting paths bounded by a perimeter path, creating four central beds and a series of borders at the base of the surrounding walls. The central beds are the main growing areas for annual crops and operate on a traditional four-course rotation of potatoes, brassicas (cabbage family), legumes (pea family), and salads and root crops, with the potato quarter being mulched with compost and dug each year as it moves around the rotation. All beds are edged with dwarf box, although there is a question mark over its long-term future as we are currently struggling with the curse of box blight, a great pity.

The wall borders accommodate perennial crops with soft fruit in the westernmost, asparagus, rhubarb, seakale and globe artichokes in the easterly, and auriculas, lily of the valley and cordon-grown gooseberries and currants in the cool, shady north-facing border. The warm south-facing border is the ideal site for bringing on early spring crops under barn cloches, herbs in early summer, and late crops such as pumpkins and gourds into the autumn. In the past the central flower border, which was a common feature of the cruciform layout, was designed for cutting for the house but is now a feature in itself, providing a blast of colour to contrast with the predominantly green vegetables from June to October. This is complemented by the Pear Tunnel on its cross axis, which adds height and structure, particularly in the naked and resolutely horizontal winter months.

Top: Glasshouses, the mushroom shed, vegetables en masse, the Lodge, the Bothy and the protective arboreal arms of garden and forestry all contribute to the feel of the walled garden.

Bottom left: No space is wasted in the kitchen garden. The narrow bed at the base of the mushroom shed wall has trained red and white currants on the wall and border auriculas in the ground, all flourishing on this shady, cool elevation.

Bottom right: Gooseberries also flourish under the same conditions.

A continuous round of successional seed sowing
both in modules and in the ground ensures continuity
of supply in the kitchen garden.

*Even after forty years of gardeniong it's still a thrill
to see your spring sowings burst into life.*

HIGH-CLASS HORTICULTURE IN A HISTORIC SETTING

Success in any venture is dependent on well-defined but not rigid objectives. For a raft of reasons, mainly in relation to available resources, hard-nosed economics and the fact that we are an arts-based institution, we decided from the outset to treat the kitchen garden mainly as a display area with a useful secondary outcome of being productive. This impacts on the planning and management of the site, so that our growing is based on longevity and beauty of display (Sarah has mounted a number of early season exhibits of individual, pot-grown vegetables under glass titled 'Vegetables are beautiful too!'), freedom from pest and disease, and only finally productivity and tastiness. Obvious expressions of this might be in the choice of, say, cabbage varieties that will stay looking good all season and that have attractive foliage both individually and when juxtaposed against other varieties. These have proved to be a favourite subject for painting classes over the years.

As in all other aspects of our management of the walled garden, our aim is not to try to emulate our forebears exactly but to continue to work within their tradition of enquiry, excellence and advancement. In the same way that the Victorian walled garden was like a mini research station pushing the boundaries in technology, growing practice and plant breeding, we like to bring the best of modern techniques to our heritage site: hence our strap line of 'High-class horticulture in a historic setting'. What we definitely do not do is restrict ourselves solely to historic varieties. If they still perform well and offer a desirable trait, then they get grown; if they do not, they are out. Over the years Sarah has developed very good contacts with the seed trade and is always keen to try worthy new varieties alongside tried and tested favourites. This has been complemented by her being the first, and so far only, woman on the RHS Vegetable Trial Committee. For nearly two decades this has been a source of never ending interest and inspiration which has resulted in us running our own trials of things like chillies, parsley, celeriac and coriander, thus stimulating the interest of both ourselves and our visitors.

PLANNING MAKES PERFECT

Alongside the glasshouses the productive garden is the area of the grounds where the pace of gardening activity and change is at its most intense. In the same way that its layout embodies structure and order, so must its management embody organization; without careful pre-season planning the growing year would soon descend into chaos and confusion. Good records are a vital tool. Planning for next year actually begins around midsummer, when the process of evaluating the current year's successes and failures starts, and then continues through to the autumn. The results are collated and stored on the computer, and are fed into the next stage of the process when the current year's plan and sowing records are reviewed in the light of the earlier performance evaluation. That information, plus any new objectives, circumstances or ideas, is taken

We do not operate a no-dig regime but our cultivation is
kept to a minimum – generally only once at the beginning
of year when the kitchen garden is cleared and prepared
for the coming season.

Many crops are sown in situ *but our brassicas would not survive the pigeons without netting.*

into account and a new growing plan produced, normally by the end of November. Then the current seed stock is reviewed and culled (seed, even if stored properly, is not viable indefinitely) and a seed order placed to match next year's requirements. When this arrives it is sorted through and put into store categorized by type, whether vegetable or flower, and then by final location and sowing date by diary week – in 2018 Week 10 starts 5 March – so that, in theory, any seed is easily found when required. Generally this works very well so that a novice can find the seed to be sown in any given week by opening the relevant week's bag, and then can access all the information they need to know for sowing and planting by referring to the planting plan and sowing book. Given the volume and complexity of the annual sowing and planting out regime, this is an essential aid.

One of the directions recorded in the sowing record is whether the subject is to be direct sown or started as a module; broadly speaking, it is a 50–50 split. As with all these things it is difficult to make completely hard and fast rules that can be applied in all conditions, which is why every site's individual sowing and growing records – which are tailored to their very particular set of circumstances – are such an important resource. Direct sowing is simple, straightforward, suits some things such as carrots, parsnips, beetroot and radish, but is very weather dependent in terms of the sowing operation itself, subsequent germination and juvenile growth. Modules are more complicated, more work, require more resources and are best reserved for subjects that mature as widely spaced individual plants such as brassicas and lettuce. The commonest problems with them is erratic watering, which can cause them to bolt, and not planting out at the optimum time. If they become overmature as a module, they will struggle to establish in the ground and, once again, tend to run up to seed. However, what they offer is every gardener's dream: total control of the growing environment at a critical period.

GROWING FRENZY

Because of our decision to treat the productive garden as a display rather than a full-on production line, we pretty well mothball it over winter. This enables us to focus on completing the extensive winter work programme that lays the foundation for next year's successful season in the arboretum, grounds and glasshouses. Then in February, as soon as we get a few dry days and soil conditions are right, we have a kitchen garden blitz. Any remnants of last year's crops and any other vegetative debris are removed, the potato quarter covered with 10 cm/4 inches of compost and then dug in, all other bare areas rotary hoed, raked out, trodden and raked over ready to go, the chip mulch on the perimeter paths renewed, the central flower border lightly mulched, and a section of the south-facing border covered with barn cloches to dry and warm the soil for our earliest sowings. And if that sounds breathless it is! Any gardener lives by the motto 'seize the day', and as the sap stirs, like Mole in *Wind in the Willows*, you can almost feel nature quivering with the urgency of it all – it is one of my favourite moments in the seasonal cycle. However, under glass the sowing cycle is already well under way, having started with

'Any gardener lives by the motto "seize the day", and as the sap stirs, like Mole in *Wind in the Willows*, you can almost feel nature quivering with the urgency of it all – it is one of my favourite moments in the seasonal cycle.'

parsley and lettuce around Christmas time, which then continues through the spring into summer. As soon as conditions are right the first outdoor sowings under the cloches are made, and then it is a question of patience until temperatures and ground conditions allow the first truly outdoor sowings of beans and peas, normally in very early March. From that point recurrent successional sowings ensure a continuous cycle of germination, growing, cropping, removal and replacement until the whole thing glides to a slow halt in the hazy, late autumn sunshine, *Deo gracias.*

Finally, two other weapons in our vegetable production armoury that offer subtle growing advantages are the large (2 m/7 ft × 20 m/66 ft) cold frame dedicated to cut-and-come-again salad leaves, baby carrots, radish and leafy herbs and various beds in the glasshouses that are used for early salad and herb production and then switch to cucumber, melon and gourd production for the summer.

THE CUTTING GARDEN

An important but often forgotten element of the high Victorian productive garden was the growing of cut flowers for the decoration of the house as it hosted a ceaseless round of balls and shooting parties. For a variety of reasons we did not originally designate a specific area for this function, intending to rely on the display borders to supply whatever was needed. However, after a year's operation we realized that the area originally set aside as a nursery in the redevelopment plan was not fit for purpose, and it was therefore converted to a cut flower area – one of those unusual 'design by cock up' outcomes that was completely successful. It consists of a series of elongated rectangular beds bisected by paths plus wall borders whose regular geometry lends itself to growing row after row of well-labelled cut flower subjects. These include herbaceous perennials, half-hardy perennials and, more unusually, a large collection of annual flowers whose polychromatic zing and ephemeral life cycle give them an especially intense presence. This vibrant diversity, presentation of the varieties as discrete subjects rather than as elements in a composition, and the ease of identification all go to make this one of the favourite areas for our garden guests.

SOFT FRUIT SMORGASBORD

Another crop that does not immediately spring to mind when thinking of the productive garden is soft fruit: as delicious to eat and expensive to source in Victorian times as it is today. We have quite a considerable area given over to the full range, including red and white currants grown as U cordons, blackcurrants as bushes, raspberry, loganberry and blackberry canes trained on a wire support framework, and strawberries both outside and under glass. As with all permanent woody plantings, the most important factors in a successful outcome are good initial soil preparation, provision of an appropriate and strong support system and appropriate pruning. Two other observations: one, we do not normally

*Top: Pear, palmette
concentrique and verrier,
two French styles of training
on the east wall of the kitchen
garden which is covered with
a variety of more unusual
trained shapes all inspired
by Le Potager du Roi at
Versailles.*

*Bottom: A view south over the
cutting garden showing the
great variety on display with a
zinnia trial in the foreground.*

*Below: Redcurrants and
white currants bejewel the
mushroom shed wall with
their glistening fruits that
surprisingly can linger all
through the summer.*

net any of our fruit. Initially we created an elaborate temporary fruit cage that we would put up and take down after harvest each year (I think fruit cages can be pretty ugly). After all that effort we still ended up with as many birds inside as out, so in the end we stopped, and in our experience we have more than enough for both us and the birds. The second is that because they are such prolific fruiters, staying on top of the harvesting can be difficult at times.

MANY HANDS . . .

In fact, harvesting tends to be the forgotten factor when people wax lyrical about the joys of the productive garden. This is probably because most of us, for most of the time, purchase our fruit and veg from the laboratory-like environs of the supermarket shelf. Here their clinically clean perfection obscures the fact that they are only there because some underpaid, overworked migrant fieldworker was labouring at dawn in a windswept Lincolnshire field to ensure a ready supply of perfect, uniform Brussels sprouts on time and keenly priced. And although on one level harvesting is the crowning glory of many months of effort, it is also fiddly, time consuming and back breaking. Without the vital support of our nimble fingered volunteers, we would struggle to harvest crops like peas, beans and soft fruit.

'If you want to be happy for an hour get drunk,
if you want to be happy for a day get married,
but if you want to be happy for life plant a garden.'
Anon.

Postscript

I opened this book by describing it, perhaps slightly whimsically at the
time, as being a record of a love affair: an infatuation with a particular
place at a particular time and shared with a particular person, my partner
in grime, Sarah. In hindsight, I can now see that description was indeed
both accurate and sincere and has been the defining characteristic of
our time at West Dean. All serious gardeners, whether professional or
amateur, may be motivated to practise their craft for a variety of reasons,
but the rock on which the edifice is built is an abiding and all-consuming
passion. To misquote Martin Luther, 'Here I kneel: I can do no other.'

Equally, I have also come to realize how much we see our working
selves as part of that rich and varied tradition, dating back to the
eighteenth century and beyond, of head gardeners who have been
the visionary custodians of some of our most lovely and significant
landscapes and gardens, arguably our greatest national contribution to
the international world of the arts. This sense of continuity over centuries
and being a link in a chain stretching back over generations has always
been most real to me as I move through the glasshouse range closing
down at the end of a busy working day. As the vents are wound shut and
the doors closed, I can almost hear the footsteps of my forebears echoing

The nurturing of West Dean Gardens has been a shared passion for twenty-seven years, a marriage made in horticultural heaven.

my actions, and though the past may be another country it still deeply informs and enriches our present day lives.

In addition, writing the book has reinforced for me how important continuity of custodianship is to the well-being of gardens. We work with a medium that has its own rhythms and timescales, not generally in step with those of the twenty-first century, but that needs to be respected to achieve the desired excellence of outcome which all real gardeners constantly strive for. Without continuity of vision and management, the garden will be unable to evolve over the timescale that the development of trees and large-scale plantings require to come to their full maturity. This has always been an elusive goal, and in reality most gardens have gone through various cycles of development, decline and renewal. No doubt this will also be true into the future, but nonetheless stability and persistence are fundamental desiderata of garden management.

However, a number of changes in the working conditions of head gardeners threaten to undermine that centuries-long tradition and break the unique relationship that such individuals have with their charges. Foremost amongst these is the demise of live-in, on-site accommodation. Historically all head gardeners (and most gardeners) lived in a house on site, often built into the walls of the walled garden. This had many practical advantages for the employer. A responsible person was always on hand to attend to any issues that occurred outside the regular working hours, particularly important with a significant unautomated glasshouse range. But far more importantly, it enabled the incumbent to develop that intimate and unique relationship with the site that only really comes with constant presence in all circumstances. The marriage analogy comes to mind again! Equally, it also facilitated the training and development of the next generation of gardeners and head gardeners, as it was relatively easy to move from one job to another because accommodation was provided. Sadly, over the last decade that tradition has pretty well disappeared from most large institutions such as the National Trust, with what would once have been 'tied' accommodation now given over to revenue-generating holiday lets or similar. Superficially this may be a rational policy, but ultimately it may have unforeseen negative impacts – in terms of recruitment and retention of committed, skilled staff – on the long-term future of those very objects the organization is there to preserve.

Of equal threat to the individuality of our garden heritage is the tendency to its homogenization. This is a process driven by the dictates of a corporate commercial mentality that denigrates the unmediated, undistracted experience of the 'genius of the place' both in and for itself and as a source of spiritual succour and imaginative nourishment. Instead it favours 'added value' initiatives such as excessive interpretation, the introduction of additional 'attractions' not grounded in the nature of the site, or a plethora of unrelated 'events'. In a world where people are gasping for authentic contact with the wellsprings of the natural world, such a policy seems perverse and unfortunate.

However, despite a few storm clouds on the horizon, I should conclude by saying that we consider ourselves to have been the most fortunate of people. To have spent one's working life in a beautiful place, doing fascinating and creative work surrounded by kind and generous people, is an enormous privilege and we have been blessed in that endeavour. May you derive as much satisfaction from your gardening lives as we have from ours.

INDEX

VISITING

ACKNOWLEDGEMENTS

West Dean Gardens is open to the public from February through to late December. Parking is free and there is a restaurant and shop on site. Continuing the rich seam of creativity, also on site is West Dean College of Arts and Conservation offering 800+ short courses as well as degrees and diplomas. Gardens and College are part of The Edward James Foundation, a charitable trust. For garden opening times, events and tickets see: www.westdeangardens.org.uk

Anna Mumford, who was foolishly persistent in trying to convince us to write a book and stuck with us when, at times, we doubted the wisdom of the enterprise.

Andrea Jones, whose pictures paint a thousand words, entrance the eye and enhance the text.

The team at Quarto: Andrew Dunn (publisher), Glenn Howard (designer) and Nancy Marten (freelance editor).

Our parents, who nurtured our nascent horticultural aspirations by letting us loose in their gardens and encouraged us to follow our instinct for outdoors over office and richness of experience over material wealth.

Our mentors who trained and cultivated us, Moira Burnett, Mike Fitt, Geoff Olive, Leo Pemberton, Peter Thoday, and our many gardening peers too numerous to mention.

Tim Heymann, Simon Ward and Alex Barron, our managers over our twenty-seven years at West Dean, who had the courage to back our vision and the wisdom to know when to apply some restraint.

And, crucially, all of the gardeners and volunteers who have worked with us over decades to make West Dean what it is today.

All photographs © Andrea Jones, except the following:

Pages 146, 154–5, 162–3, 164, 165, 180 (bottom right, above and below), 184, 196–7, 228 (top), 270, 274–5, 281 © Trevor Sims

Pages 149, 150 (top left, above and below, and top right), 152 (bottom) © Jim Buckland

Page 283 © Charlie Hopkinson

At West Dean: The Creation of an Exemplary Garden

First published in 2018 by White Lion Publishing,
an imprint of The Quarto Group.
The Old Brewery, 6 Blundell Street,
London N7 9BH, United Kingdom.
T (0)20 7700 6700 F (0)20 7700 8066
www.QuartoKnows.com

A catalogue record for this book is available from
the British Library.

ISBN 978-0-7112-3892-3

10 9 8 7 6 5 4 3 2

Designed by Glenn Howard
Printed in China

Brimming with creative inspiration, how-to projects and useful
information to enrich your everyday life, Quarto Knows is a favourite
destination for those pursuing their interests and passions. Visit our
site and dig deeper with our books into your area of interest: Quarto
Creates, Quarto Cooks, Quarto Homes, Quarto Lives, Quarto Drives,
Quarto Explores, Quarto Gifts, or Quarto Kids.